If Not for the Grace of God
Study Guide

by
Joyce Meyer

Harrison House
Tulsa, Oklahoma

If Not for the Grace of God Study Guide
ISBN 1-57794-447-X
Copyright © 2002 by Joyce Meyer
Life In The Word, Inc.
P. O. Box 655
Fenton, Missouri 63026

Published by Harrison House, Inc.
P. O. Box 35035
Tulsa, Oklahoma 74153

06 05 04 03 02   15 14 13 12 11 10 9 8 7 6 5 4 3 2 1

Contents

Introduction

God wants to give us His grace to provide us with the power to have an enjoyable life. Grace is so much more than God's unmerited favor. It is the power and ability of God available to meet all of our needs without any cost to us. We cannot earn grace, and it is not deserved; it is freely given to us by God through His Son Jesus Christ.[1] We receive it through faith and by humbling ourselves before the Lord, casting all our cares upon Him and trusting Him to take care of them as He has promised in His Word.

Grace is simple, which is why many people miss it. They find it difficult to understand, and they tend to overlook it and try to handle everything themselves by their own power and in their own way. In doing so they muddle through life and fail to tap into the blessings God has for them.

If you will resist taking matters into your own hands and not labor to bring forth your own results but depend entirely upon the grace of God, you will enjoy more results than those who wear themselves out trying to produce by their own effort.

For many years I depended on myself most of the time. My life was filled with dead works — my plans, my ideas, my efforts being expended trying to make things happen in my life. I admit those were frustrating, miserable years. Then the Lord opened to me a whole new realm of revelation about His marvelous grace. I came to realize that His grace was available to me to make the needed changes in my life, that just as I received my salvation by grace through faith, I needed to trust and receive every other blessing from God in the same way. When I understood that truth, I began to enjoy the full benefits of grace in my daily life.

A solid understanding of the grace of God is essential to living a victorious life. As you work through this study guide, you will come to understand the role and function of grace in the life of the believer. The revelation of God's grace is transforming. With this new knowledge, I believe that the burden of works of the flesh, of human effort, will begin to lift off your shoulders, and you will exchange trying for trusting, striving for resting and experience real success as you humbly lean on God.

USING THIS STUDY GUIDE

The purpose of this workbook is to reinforce the principles taught in my book, *If Not for the Grace of God*. You will need a copy of *If Not for the Grace of God* to work through this book.

This study guide is written in a question and answer format. By reading a chapter in *If Not for the Grace of God*, studying the designated Scripture verses and answering the questions in the corresponding chapter of the study guide, you will gain a deeper understanding of the principles and learn more easily how to incorporate them into your daily life.

To use this workbook, look up and read the corresponding chapter in *If Not for the Grace of God*. Next look up in your Bible the Scriptures designated in the study guide and read them. This is an important step because those Scriptures are the basis of the teaching in that particular chapter and are taken directly from that chapter.

Answer the questions in the study guide by referring to the appropriate chapter in *If Not for the Grace of God*. Once you have finished answering the questions in each chapter, turn to the answer key in the back of this book to check your answers.

1. Work at a comfortable pace. Don't rush to finish quickly. Stay in each chapter until you have a thorough understanding of the material and how it pertains to your life.

2. Follow these steps with each chapter in this study guide.

3. Use this study guide for individual study or group discussion. When using it in a group, discuss your answers and learn how to apply the principles in a way that may not have occurred to you until you heard the experiences of others.

Consistently and steadily working through this book will help you learn how to live by grace and be free from the frustration of trying hard but failing often. When you are doing all you know to do and not getting any results, it always ends in frustration. But living by grace is a whole new way of living that makes the power of God available to you to change things in your life that you thought you would have to live with forever.

GRACE MAKES THE IMPOSSIBLE POSSIBLE

"... apart from Me [cut off from vital union with Me] you can do nothing."

John 15:5

Grace is not us doing anything; it is us believing and letting God do things through us that only He can do. Once we understand grace, we must grow in learning how to receive it in every situation — totally trusting in God is something we grow into. This does not mean that we should never make any effort to achieve or accomplish anything in life. But we should not attempt anything without asking God for help and leaning on Him all the way through.

As we learn to commit our lives to God, trusting ourselves to Him in everything and for everything, relying not upon our faith but upon His grace, we will be filled with His rest and His peace. The more we relax and put our trust in God, the more we will experience His best for us and be full of gratitude and thanksgiving for what He accomplishes in and through us that we don't deserve for Him to do.

It is my sincere prayer that working through this study guide, along with the book, *If Not for the Grace of God,* will help firmly establish in your heart forever that as long as you try to do everything yourself, you will be frustrated and depressed because you are trying to do God's job, but if you allow the grace of God to have full reign in your life, nothing will be impossible to you!

1. How does the author define grace?_____
   _____
   _____.

2. How is grace received? _____
   _____
   _____.

3. Upon what must all knowledge of faith be built?_____
   _____.

4. a. There is nothing more powerful than grace. What does the author say is based upon it? _____

_____

_____

_____.

b. What are we like without grace? _____

_____

_____.

c. What would be the result in our life if it were not for the grace of God?_____

_____.

5. Read Luke 2:40

a. According to this verse, what happened to Jesus as a child? __

_____

_____

_____

_____.

b. This verse contains everything we need to be happy, healthy, prosperous and successful in our Christian walk. In reality what is the one thing that we need?_____

_____

_____

_____.

c. What will happen to us if we allow the grace of God to have full reign in our life? What happens to us without that grace?____

_____

_____.

d. What is the only way we can do all things through Christ Who strengthens us? _____

_____.

6. Read Ephesians 2:10; Hebrews 4:3; John 15:5

a. In your own words describe what Paul tells us about ourselves in Ephesians 2:10: _____

_____

_____

_____

_____

_____

_____

_____.

b. What does the writer of Hebrews tell us about our works? ___

_____

_____.

c. Based on Ephesians 2:10 and Hebrews 4:3, why must we stop talking about "our" ministry, as though it is something we undertake on our own initiative or carry out by our own ability? ___

_____

_____

_____.

d. What does Jesus tell us in John 15:5? _____

_____.

e. What is meant by the author's statement that we "are the vessels through which God does His own works"? _____

_____
_____
_____.

f. What will be the result if we really believe that God is in complete control of our life? Why? _____

_____
_____
_____
_____
_____
_____.

g. Everything in our lives depends, not upon our merits or abilities or works, but upon God's grace, which is His_____

_____
_____.

h. If you have needs today, what should you do? What will be the result?_____

_____
_____
_____
_____
_____
_____
_____
_____

As followers of Jesus Christ, that is our _____

_____ and _____.

d. How can we get into conflict by wanting something that is clearly God's will for us? _____

_____.

5. Read James 4:2; Psalm 31:15; John 16:24 KJV

a. According to James 4:2, how does God refer to jealousy and envy?_____.

b. In that passage, what does the Bible say about hating others because of their special gifts? _____

_____

_____.

c. God may call a person to do something, and then not allow him to do it for a while. And he will never be able to do it, until he _____

_____

_____.

d. According to the last sentence in verse 2 of James 4, why do we not have the things we desire? _____

_____.

e. According to John 16:24 KJV, what is the one thing we are to do instead of complaining about our problems and spending half our time trying to figure out what we can do to solve them?_____

_____. Why don't we do that?

_____
_____.

f. What is one reason we are not more successful than we are in our walk of faith? _____
_____
_____.

g. What must we do in order for God to give us what we need by His grace?_____
_____
_____
_____.

6. Read James 4:3

a. In this study, what word does the author hope to eradicate from our vocabulary?_____. What word does she say should replace it?_____.

b. According to James 4:3, rather than setting out to acquire the things we need or desire, we are to ask for them. Why do we often not receive from God what we ask for? _____
_____
_____.

c. Sometimes the thing we are asking God for is not wrong in itself, but He cannot grant our request yet because_____
_____
_____.

f. God knows what we are facing in every situation of life, and He will work out things for the best, if we will _____ _____.

11. Read 1 Peter 5:5 WORRELL; 1 Peter 5:5

a. In both of these versions of 1 Peter 5:5 we see that God sets Himself against the _____, but gives grace to the _____.

b. It is always _____ that is our motivator when we try to handle our own situations rather than humbling ourselves and asking God what we ought to do — and then being _____ enough to do what He says, whether we agree with it or not, whether we like it or not.

c. What is the difference between trying to use what we think is faith to make our plans work and relying on grace to allow God to work out His plan? _____ _____ _____.

d. Why is it scriptural to say that God sometimes frustrates people? _____ _____ _____ _____.

e. Who are these people? _____ _____ _____

_____

_____

_____

_____

_____

_____

_____

_____

_____

_____.

f. Why does the Bible say that God opposes us when we act in
    pride?_____

    _____

    _____.

12. Read 1 Peter 5:6

What does it mean to humble yourself under the mighty hand of
God that in due time He may exalt you? _____

_____

_____

_____

_____

_____

_____.

13. Read 1 Peter 5:7; 1 John 4:18 KJV

a. Why will the person who really understands the grace of God
    not worry?_____

17. Read Acts 2:27; Galatians 2:21

    a. The verse in Acts 2:27 is a prophetic utterance that came forth from King David referring to the Messiah. Based on this passage, what was the attitude of Jesus?_____
    _____
    _____.

    b. What carries us through the hard times, as we wait patiently for the grace of God to work out our deliverance? _____
    _____.

    c. Although faith is important, it is not the actual power that delivers. What then does faith do for us in time of trial? ___
    _____
    _____
    _____
    _____.

    d. What is the danger of keeping our faith on the line, of keeping on believing that what we need we are going to get by faith? _____
    _____.

    e. What must we do to avoid this danger? Why? _____
    _____
    _____
    _____.

    f. What is the danger in focusing so much on believing?_____
    _____
    _____

_____
_____.

   g. What happens if we place too much emphasis on our faith —
on our belief and our faithfulness? _____
_____
_____.

   h. What must we do to avoid this danger and overemphasis? _____
_____
_____
_____
_____
_____
_____
_____.

18.   Read Acts 2:28-33; Romans 8:11 KJV; Hebrews 10:23

   a. In this passage in Acts, what did Peter tell the crowd assembled in Jerusalem on the Day of Pentecost? _____
_____
_____
_____
_____
_____.

The Power of Grace

As with the previous chapter, before answering the questions below, first read the corresponding chapter in *If Not for the Grace of God* then the Scriptures designated below. After you complete the chapter, check the answer key in the back of this book.

To gain the greatest benefit from this workbook, continue using this method throughout.

1. Read Ezra 4:1-5; John 16:33 KJV; John 15:18,20

    a. What is the author's message in this chapter about? _____
        _____.

    b. According to Ezra 4:1-5, when the Israelites began building the temple, who came and asked to join them because they claimed they worshipped the same God? _____
        _____.

    c. What happened when the Israelites told these people they had no part in building a temple to the Lord? _____
        _____
        _____
        _____.

    d. According to John 16:33 KJV and John 15:18,20, why are we wrong if we think we can do anything for God without stirring up trouble for ourselves? _____
        _____
        _____

_____
_____.

e. Although we know that we cannot go through life on this earth without encountering some kind of trouble, what does trouble often do to us when we do encounter it? _____
_____
_____.

f. What can happen to people who come to the Lord and then suddenly begin to be attacked in ways that are totally different from anything they have experienced before, if they don't have proper instruction in this area? _____
_____
_____.

g. What mistake do we often make when our enemy, Satan, comes against us? _____
_____.

What is wrong with this use of faith? _____
_____.

h. What is the purpose of faith? Why? _____
_____
_____
_____.

i. What is one of the best ways of standing our ground, backing the devil off our property and driving him out of different areas in our life? _____
_____.

j. What should you do once you have gained a victory over the enemy? Why? _____

_____

_____ .

k. What does the full-time job of being a victorious Christian require us to do? _____

_____ .

l. Like the Israelites who were building the temple in the story in Ezra chapter 4, what must we be ready to do? _____

_____

_____ .

2. Read Zechariah 4:1-3; review James 4:6

a. Based on Zechariah 4:1-3, describe what Zechariah saw in the vision in which an angel spoke to him. _____

_____

_____

_____

_____ .

b. In the Word of God, what does oil represent? _____

_____ .

c. What is the Holy Spirit? _____

_____ .

d. James 4:6 tells us that the grace of God is the _____

_____

_____ .

According to the author, what does that mean?_____

_____

_____.

3. Read Zechariah 4:4-6

    a. According to verse 6 of this passage, what was the word of the
        Lord to Zerubbabel? _____

    _____

    _____.

    b. Here the Lord is speaking to the same people who were try-
        ing to build the temple in the book of Ezra. What is He telling
        them?_____

    _____

    _____

    _____

    _____

    _____

    _____.

4. Read Zechariah 4:7

    a. The Samaritans who came against the Israelites as they were
        building the temple of the Lord had become like what to
        them?_____

    _____

    _____.

    b. If you feel that the Lord has told you to do something, but
        that the enemy has thrown up a mountain in your path to
        frustrate you and prevent you from carrying out the Lord's

will, the problem you are facing in that situation is one of

_____.

Why? _____

_____

_____

_____.

c. As believers, we are not to have our eyes focused on _____
    _____, but on _____
    _____.

d. What happens when we give in to the temptation to get
    caught up in the problem, to get into reasoning and figuring
    and worrying? _____
    _____.

e. How can you make all your mountains become molehills?
    _____
    _____
    _____.

f. If God has told you to do something, you will never _____
    _____ if you don't understand
    _____.

g. It is not by power or by might that we win the victory over
    our enemy, but by _____.

h. We overcome through _____,
    by _____.

5. Review Ephesians 2:8,9; read Hebrews 11:6 KJV

    a. We must understand that faith is not the power that saves us, it is simply_____
    _____
    _____.

    b. Why do principles, methods and formulas have no real power?_____
    _____.

    c. What does Hebrews 11:6 KJV tell us about faith? _____
    _____
    _____.

    d. Why is faith so important and so vital? _____
    _____
    _____
    _____.

    e. Why has God spent the past several years training His people in faith? _____
    _____
    _____.

    f. In all of our spiritual activity (prayer, praise, meditation on the Word, Bible study, confession, spiritual warfare, etc.), we must be careful that we don't start worshipping — adhering to, trusting in and relying on — _____
    _____.

g. It is possible to develop faith in our _____ rather than faith in our _____.

h. Why is this almost frightening? _____ _____.

i. As good as all these things are, they are of no good to us whatsoever unless_____ _____.

6. a. If you are a frustrated, confused Christian, what is your problem? _____.

b. If you are plugged in, if you are _____ _____, then you know that it is not by your might or power, but by _____ _____.

c. When we try to make things happen by our own strength and effort, we become frustrated and confused in the process. We may be trying to move mountains by our human effort, but what should we be doing? _____ _____.

d. Frustration is not part of our divine inheritance, and neither is _____.

e. We will never accomplish anything unless we are plugged into the divine power source. How do we stay plugged in? Through a _____ — which requires _____.

f. The victory is not in methods; it is in _____.
    If we are to live victoriously, we are going to have to _____
    _____
    _____ and find _____
    _____.

g. God has a personalized plan for each of us, a plan that will
    lead us to victory. Why are principles, formulas and methods
    not the ultimate answer to our problems as individuals? _____
    _____
    _____
    _____.

h. As good as all these things may be as general guidelines, they
    are no substitute for _____
    _____.

7. Read 1 Samuel 17:26; Ephesians 6:10-17 KJV; Matthew 25:1-12

    a. The Source of all peace and victory is not the things of God,
        but _____.

    b. If the devil tries to keep people out of anything, it is _____
        _____.

    c. According to Ephesians 6:10 KJV, as soldiers of the Cross, we
        are not supposed to be afraid of our enemy, the devil. Instead,
        we are to _____
        _____.

d. The devil comes against _____
_____
_____ .

e. Based on Ephesians 6:13-17 KJV, how do we withstand the
devil? _____
_____
_____
_____ .

f. All of that armor and all of those weapons come from _____
_____ .

g. Based on Ephesians 6:10,11 KJV, when is the only time we
can properly wear the armor of God? _____
_____ .

h. We must learn that it is only in the _____
of the Lord that we receive the _____
of the Lord.

i. Like anything worthwhile, sitting quietly in the presence of
the Lord takes time to master. And it is not something that we
can learn from someone else. Why is it not possible to teach
another human being to fellowship with God? _____
_____
_____ .

j. Why must you sometimes spend more time in fellowship
with God than your usual day by day fellowship with Him?
_____
_____ .

k. Where does the abundant, enjoyable, victorious life God wants us to have come from? _____ _____.

l. _____ with God privately before you _____ publicly. Spend time with God so you can _____ _____.

8. Read Galatians 2:20 KJV

a. The devil wants us to think that we can buy the grace of God. But God's grace is not for sale, because by its very definition — _____ — it is a _____.

b. Grace cannot be bought by prayer, good works, Bible reading or offerings. It cannot be bought by reading, memorizing or confessing Scriptures. It cannot even be bought by faith. It is receivable, but it is not _____.

c. If we Christians want to act better, we have got to be _____ the Spirit of the Living God. If we want to shine, we have got to _____ _____.

d. According to Galatians 2:20 KJV, the success of our life and ministry does not depend upon our effort, but upon _____ _____ _____ _____.

e. In our zeal to serve the Lord, why is it that sometimes despite all our activity nothing happens? _____

_____

_____.

f. Even when God does show up and work in and through us, what mistake do we sometimes make?_____

_____

_____.

9. Read Romans 4:4,5; Isaiah 64:6 KJV; Mark 4:27 KJV

a. Based on Romans 4:4,5, in your own words describe the difference between a laborer and a believer: _____

_____

_____

_____

_____

_____

_____

_____

_____.

b. What is wrong with reading the Bible, praying, meditating, making a positive confession or even being with the Lord, in an effort to get something from Him?_____

_____

_____.

c. We must be very careful that even when we operate by all the right methods our motives are pure. Why? _____

_____
_____.

d. According to the Bible, what do we deserve?_____
_____.

Based on Isaiah 64:6 KJV, why do we deserve that?_____
_____
_____
_____.

e. What happens if we look upon our righteousness as com-
pared with the righteousness of Almighty God, instead of
comparing our righteousness with the unrighteousness of
others? _____
_____
_____.

f. What should be our only reason for seeking the Lord and fellowshipping with Him? _____
_____.

g. What does the saying "Farmers have formulas for planting,
but not for reaping" mean? _____
_____
_____.

h. In Mark 4:27 KJV, to what does Jesus liken the Kingdom of
God? _____
_____
_____
_____.

    i.   None of the good seed we plant, such as prayer, Bible study, preparation, meditation, a good confession, an offering, church attendance, good works and time spent with God, is a way of purchasing God's grace. Why? _____

_____

_____.

    j.   How then do God's blessings come upon us? _____

_____.

10.   Read Mark 11:22,23

    a.   In this passage, what is the first thing Jesus tells us to do?

_____.

    b.   If we are wrapped up in faith and confession, what mistake can we make? _____

_____

_____.

    c.   In order to receive anything from God we have to _____

_____

_____.

    d.   We confess the Word, God works through it, and our faith

_____.

11.   Read Ephesians 3:20 KJV

    a.   What does this verse tell us about God? _____

_____

_____.

b. Our job is to do the asking, in faith, in trust. That opens the channel. But it is God Who does the work, not us. According to this verse, how does He do it? _____
_____.

c. Whatever we receive from the Lord is directly related to what? _____.

d. Why does the Lord Himself sometimes not let us change?__
_____
_____.

e. We humans do not deserve the least of God's blessings. Once we fully understand that truth, then _____
_____
_____.

12. Read Galatians 3:2-5

a. In verse 2 of this passage, what does Paul ask the Galatian believers?_____
_____
_____?

b. What does he ask them in verse 3?_____
_____
_____?

c. What is the third question Paul asks the Galatians in this passage? _____
_____
_____?

d. What is Paul's concluding question?_____

_____

_____

_____?

e. If we are frustrated and confused about trying to change ourselves, what should we do? _____

_____.

f. What is it about the Lord that we often have to learn the hard
way? _____

_____.

g. God is the only One Who can _____

_____.

h. Many times we will ask for God's help only if we think ____

_____

_____.

i. Why does God sometimes prevent your efforts to change
from working for you?_____

_____.

j. We need to learn to ask the Lord for help instead of _____

_____

_____.

13. Read 2 Corinthians 3:17,18

a. Based on this passage, where does our liberty, our emancipa-
tion, our freedom from bondage, come from? _____

_____

_____.

   b. How does it come? _____

_____.

   c. Whose credit is it? _____.

14.   Read Philippians 1:6

   a. Who has begun this good work in us? _____.

   b. What will bring us into God's rest? _____

_____.

   c. Once we have His rest and peace, what can we do? _____

_____.

15.   Read Hebrews 12:2; Hebrews 6:12

   a. Based on Hebrews 12:2, what does the author encourage you to do with your eyes? _____

_____

_____.

   b. Why are you to do that? _____

_____

_____

_____

_____

_____

_____.

c. What do people do many times once they get into the Word of God and come under conviction?_____

_____

_____

_____

_____

_____

_____.

d. Why is that a mistake?_____

_____

_____.

e. What do we have to do to be changed by God? _____

_____

_____

_____.

f. According to Hebrews 6:12, how do we receive the promises of God?_____.

16. Read 1 Thessalonians 5:22-24

a. In verse 23 of this passage, what does the word *sanctify* mean? _____.

b. Who does this? _____.

c. Verse 24 tells us that God Who called us to Himself is faithful and utterly trustworthy and that He will do it. What will He do? _____

_____
_____.

d. First Paul says in verse 22 that we are to abstain from evil, and then in the very next verse he turns right around and says that the Lord will do it for us. In that case, what is our part? _____!

e. What is one of the blessings that we receive through the channel of faith? _____
_____.

f. Why do we sing, "To God be the glory, great things He hath done"? _____
_____
_____
_____.

17. Read John 6:27-29

a. In this passage, what was wrong with the people wanting to know what they must do to work the works of God? _____
_____
_____
_____.

b. How are we the same way those people were? _____
_____
_____
_____.

c. In verse 29 what was Jesus' answer to those people? _____

_____

_____ .

d. We are supposed to be achievers, but what is the way we achieve? Why? _____

_____ .

Freedom From Worry and Reasoning

1. Read John 14:27

    a. According to such Scriptures as this one, what does God want for His children? _____
    _____.

    b. According to the dictionary, what does "worry" mean? _____
    _____
    _____
    _____
    _____.

    c. What is another dictionary definition of this word that is worth pondering? _____
    _____.

    d. How does this second definition apply to the spiritual realm?
    _____
    _____
    _____
    _____.

    e. So worry is not just something we do to ourselves, it is also something _____
    _____.

    f. What is the author's definition of "reasoning"? _____
    _____
    _____

_____
_____.

g. In what way can reasoning seem different than worry? _____
_____
_____
_____
_____
_____.

h. How can reasoning seem to be positive and productive? ___
_____
_____
_____
_____
_____.

i. The kind of peace that comes from reasoning is usually a _____
_____ peace that doesn't last, because we are
_____
_____.

2. Read Proverbs 3:5-7; Proverbs 16:9; Ephesians 5:17

a. What does the writer of Proverbs mean when he tells us in
Proverbs 3:7 not to be wise in our own eyes? _____
_____
_____
_____.

b. Based on Proverbs 16:9 and Ephesians 5:17, there is no argu-
ment that we need to plan. The problem is not in our planning,

but in our _____

_____.

3. Read Hebrews 12:14 KJV

    a. _____ is the devil's playground!

    b. Often our problem is not _____ planning, but _____ planning.

    c. In regard to planning, when do we become excessive? _____

    _____

    _____

    _____

    _____

    _____

    _____.

    d. How can you know when you have gone from normal planning and preparing to worrying and reasoning? _____

    _____

    _____.

    e. Every time you feel frustrated and confused, it is a sign that you are _____

    _____.

    f. The more you worry and reason, the more you fret and strain and turn the problem over in your mind, the more _____

    _____.

    g. In Hebrews 12:14 KJV, what does the Word of God say we are to do? _____.

    h. What is wrong with reasoning? _____

_____

_____ .

4.   Read Colossians 3:15

    a. What does this verse say to do about peace? _____

_____

_____

_____

_____ .

    b. In this regard, what does the flesh enjoy? _____

_____

_____ .

    c. The author says that she used to start out every day by sitting down with a cup of coffee and fellowshipping with her problems. Are you fellowshipping with your problems, or with the Lord? Are you into works, or grace?_____

_____

_____ .

5.   Read Romans 11:6 KJV; Ephesians 3:16 KJV; 1 Corinthians 14:33 KJV; review Zechariah 4:6,7

    a. What is the Apostle Paul telling us in Romans 11:6 KJV? _____

_____

_____

_____ .

b. Stated another way, grace and works are _____
_____. Where one exists,
_____.

c. Anytime we get into works, what happens? Why? _____
_____
_____
_____
_____
_____.

d. Why do we only get more and more frustrated and confused
as long as we continue to try to figure out our own problems? _____
_____.

e. In the author's ministry, what prayer request does she receive
most often? _____.

f. According to Ephesians 3:16 KJV, where does discernment
come from? _____.

g. How does the author define discernment? _____
_____
_____
_____.

h. How do we know that confusion is not from God? _____
_____.

i. What happens once you turn from your reasoning to the
grace of God? _____

_____

_____

_____.

j. Based on Zechariah 4:7, we are not to try to wear down a mountain of human obstacles with a hammer, but we are to

_____

_____.

k. Where _____ fail, _____ always succeeds.

6. Read Ephesians 6:11-17; review Ephesians 6:10 KJV; read 1 John 4:4 KJV; Proverbs 18:14; James 1:5-7; review John 6:29

a. What should you do when the mountain you face seems to be bigger than God? _____

_____.

b. What does God mean when He says that He wants us to face the mountain?_____

_____

_____.

c. When you grow to the point that you have no fear of the enemy or his works, you won't be afraid of the devil or the problems he causes, because you know that _____

_____

_____.

d. Why should we not always try to avoid obstacles or constantly run away from the things that oppose us? _____

_____

_____

_____

_____

_____.

e. In Ephesians 6:11-17, we are told to put on the whole armor of God. Why is there no part of the armor to cover our backs?

_____

_____

_____.

f. We are not supposed to turn tail and run from the enemy. Instead, we are to _____

_____

_____

_____

_____.

g. We may not know what the answer to our problem is, but we know _____

_____.

h. Too often people run to each other for answers instead of running to the Lord. When you have a problem, do you run to the phone or to the throne? _____

_____.

11. Read Ephesians 2:10; 2 Corinthians 12:9 KJV

a. Why it is hard for us to enjoy life if we don't have assurance about today, peace about yesterday and confidence about tomorrow? _____

_____

_____

_____ .

b. If we have enough faith, won't we get to the point where that is not the case? _____

_____

_____

_____

_____ .

c. How will God see to it that we are always dependent upon Him? _____

_____ .

d. Although we may get worried, why does God never get worried? _____

_____

_____ .

e. God won't give us all the answers today that we will need tomorrow. With each new day comes _____

_____ that we need to live

that day and meet the challenges of it.

f. No matter what happens, God is still in control. He has _____

_____ to _____

_____ in this
life. And His _____ is _____
to meet all our needs.

12.   Read Hebrews 4:16

   a. Although God has mountains of grace, He doesn't waste it.
       Why not?_____

       _____

       _____.

   b. Based on this passage, when do we get God's grace, His
       power?_____

       _____.

   c. Why do we have to have faith and keep continually seeking
       God? _____

       _____

       _____.

   d. Another interesting point about grace, besides the fact that
       God does not waste it, is that it can be _____

       _____ or _____

       according to the need.

   e. Right now you may be finding yourself in desperate need of
       a richer, fuller measure of God's abiding grace. If so, what
       should you do? _____

       _____

       _____

       _____.

13. a. There are several things that can keep us from receiving the grace of God. One of these is ignorance, not knowing enough to call on the Lord, asking Him to pour out His grace in time of need. Another is _____ _____.

     b. _____ and grace do not mix.

     c. There is also no way to receive God's grace while seeking _____ from others or fellowshipping with _____.

     d. God never leads us where He cannot _____ us.

14. a. According to the prophecy the author received from the Lord, what does His grace require us to do? _____ _____ _____ _____.

     b. According to that prophecy, where did the ideas, the hopes, the dreams that are inside us originate? _____ _____ _____.

     c. It is not our job to bring them to pass; it is our job to _____ _____ _____.

15. What reason does the Lord give in the prophecy for our experiencing so many ups and downs? _____ _____

_____

_____

_____.

16. a. Why do we need God's grace to be emptied of human effort, the cares of daily living and fleshly frustrations? _____

_____.

   b. What is the only way we can escape from dependence on our works? _____.

17. Read Romans 5:20 KJV; Luke 18:27; Philippians 4:13; Isaiah 41:10

   a. Once we learn how to receive grace, what will be the result? Why? _____

_____

_____

_____.

   b. What happens if our problem gets bigger and multiplies? _____

_____

_____

_____

_____

_____

_____.

   c. What is impossible with man is _____.

   d. According to Philippians 4:13, we can do _____ things through Christ Who strengthens us.

18. Read Matthew 11:28 KJV; Revelation 3:6,13 KJV

    a. What is another definition of grace given in this prophecy?
    _____.

    b. What will be the result of God's grace and power flowing through us? _____
    _____
    _____
    _____
    _____
    _____
    _____
    _____.

    c. After having re-read the prophecy, are you receiving the grace of God that is available to you? _____
    _____.

19. Read 1 Corinthians 2:2 KJV; Ecclesiastes 12:12; 1 Corinthians 8:1; 1 Corinthians 2:14 KJV

    a. We try to know everything, but Paul did just the opposite. According to 1 Corinthians 2:2 KJV, what did he try to do?
    _____
    _____
    _____.

    b. Unlike us, who worry about all the things we don't know, Paul was trying to get rid of some of the things he did know. Based on Ecclesiastes 12:12 and 1 Corinthians 8:1, why did he do that? _____

_____

_____

_____

_____

_____ .

c. What was Paul referring to when he said that he had determined to know nothing but Jesus Christ, and Him crucified?

_____

_____ .

20. Read Romans 8:6

a. According to this verse, how many minds are there? What are
they? _____

_____ .

b. That doesn't mean that we have two brains, it simply means
that _____

_____ .

c. From what two sources do we get information, and how do
they operate? _____

_____

_____

_____

_____

_____

_____ .

21. Read 1 Corinthians 2:16; Romans 8:14; Galatians 5:18

    a. According to 1 Corinthians 2:16, what do we have and what does that mean? _____ _____ _____.

    b. In spite of this truth in 1 Corinthians 2:16, how do many of us live our lives most of the time? _____ _____.

    c. In Romans 8:14 and Galatians 5:18, what does the Bible say about how we are to be led? _____ _____ _____.

    d. When are we treading on dangerous ground in this area? Why? _____ _____ _____ _____ _____.

    e. First Corinthians 2:16 tells us that because the Holy Spirit lives in us, we have the mind of Christ, but what is the problem? _____ _____ _____ _____ _____

_____
_____ .

f. How then must we learn to live? _____
_____ .

22. Read Proverbs 23:7 KJV; James 1:8 KJV

a. When does the devil like to attack us? _____
_____
_____
_____ .

b. What important principle does that illustrate? _____
_____
_____ .

c. Evil spirits constantly bombard us with negative thoughts. What happens if we receive those negative thoughts and dwell on them? Why? _____
_____
_____ .

d. What happens if we accept the lies of the devil as reality?
_____
_____ .

e. What should we do in moments of worry, stress and turmoil? Why? _____
_____
_____
_____

_____

_____.

f. What are the two vats of information that we have within us, and how are they different? _____

_____

_____

_____

_____.

g. It is up to us to decide which source we are going to drink from. In James 1:8 KJV, what does the Bible call the practice of trying to drink from both sources? _____

_____.

h. What does this mean? _____

_____

_____

_____.

i. What must we do if we are ever going to live the happy, victorious and successful Christian life the Lord wills for us?

_____

_____

_____

_____

_____.

Supernatural Favor

1. Read Genesis 39:20-23; Luke 2:52

    a. Based on these two passages, what lesson does God want us to learn from the example of Joseph and others in the Bible?

    _____

    _____

    _____.

    b. As children of God, favor is available to us. Why is it then that we never receive and enjoy favor and all the other good things the Lord makes available to us? _____

    _____

    _____.

    c. God wants to give you favor, just as He gave favor to Joseph. What must you do in order to receive that favor? _____

    _____

    _____.

    d. What kind of attitude did Joseph have and maintain that allowed God to give him favor? _____

    _____

    _____.

2. Read Esther 2:15-17; 1 Samuel 2:7

    a. What Scripture in the Bible says that God brings one person down and lifts up another?_____.

b. Why did God raise up Esther from obscurity to become the queen of the entire land and give her favor with everyone she met, including the king? _____ _____.

c. Why was Esther not afraid to go to the king and ask him to intervene on behalf of herself and her people, even though to do so could have cost her her very life? _____ _____ _____.

d. If you find yourself in a situation in which you are being harassed, persecuted or discriminated against, what should you do? Why?_____ _____ _____ _____.

e. Instead of going through life being afraid that nobody likes you and harboring a fear of rejection, what should you do? _____ _____ _____ _____.

3. a. Trying to get favor on your own is not only hard work; it is often pointless. Why?_____ _____ _____.

b. The problem with that is that you are trying to _____
    _____.

c. Favor is a part of _____.

d. How are "grace" and "favor" related? _____
    _____
    _____
    _____
    _____.

e. What then is the favor or grace of God? _____
    _____
    _____
    _____
    _____
    _____
    _____.

f. If one of the twenty-five names of the Holy Spirit found in the
    Bible is "the Spirit of grace," how do we find favor with God
    and with man? _____.

g. Grace is the power of God coming to us through the channel
    of our faith, but in a very specific area. What then is favor?
    _____
    _____
    _____.

h. Once you believe God for supernatural favor, what does it do
    for you? _____
    _____.

4.   Read James 4:6

a.   What is the difference between natural favor and supernatural favor? _____
_____.

b.   Why doesn't God want us to spend our time and energy trying to earn favor with Him or others? _____
_____
_____
_____.

c.   What kind of favor does God want us to have, and how do we get it? _____
_____
_____
_____.

d.   What is another reason why we are not to spend our time and energy seeking natural favor? _____
_____.

e.   If you get acceptance with people by your own works, you must _____
_____.

f.   Why should we pray daily for supernatural favor? _____
_____
_____
_____
_____.

g. What happens whenever we quit trying to do it ourselves and start allowing the Lord to give us His favor? _____

_____

_____.

h. What is one reason why the Lord resists the proud, but gives grace (unmerited, supernatural favor) to the humble, as stated in James 4:6? _____

_____

_____

_____

_____.

5. Read Daniel 1:1-3,6-9

a. According to this passage, why did the chief of the eunuchs agree to allow Daniel and his friends to follow their own diet and not the king's rich diet as long as it didn't harm them?

_____

_____

_____

_____.

b. Why did Daniel eventually rise to become prime minister of Babylon, then the world's greatest power, and his three friends to become high officials in the kingdom? _____

_____

_____.

c. Do you think that would have happened if Daniel and the Hebrew children had tried to promote themselves by seeking natural favor? _____.

6. Read Luke 2:52; John 7:32,45,46; Matthew 27:19; Matthew 27:24; Luke 23:47,48

   a. According to Luke 2:52, in what ways did Jesus increase?

   _____

   _____

   _____.

   b. Even those who did not believe in Jesus recognized that He enjoyed favor with God and with men. In John chapter 7, when the Pharisees sent guards to arrest Jesus because He was claiming to be the Son of God, the guards went back empty-handed, saying, _____

   _____!

   c. According to Matthew 27:19, even as Jesus was being judged, what message did Pilate's wife send to him to indicate that she also recognized Jesus for Who He was, the Christ, the anointed — the favored — of God? _____

   _____.

   d. Pilate himself feared Jesus because he also recognized God's favor on Him. In Matthew 27:24 what did Pilate publicly declare to try to excuse himself while washing his hands before the mob? _____

   _____

   _____.

e. According to Luke 23:47, after Jesus was crucified, what did the Roman centurion in charge of the crucifixion say about Jesus to indicate that he recognized Him for Who He really was? _____

_____

_____!

f. So Jesus found favor with God and men not only as He grew to manhood, but all through His life — and even _____

_____.

g. How would the author like for us to come to see ourselves?

_____.

h. How does God see us in a different light from the way we see ourselves? _____

_____

_____

_____

_____

_____

_____.

i. What is the reason God sees us this way? _____

_____

_____

_____.

j. Why should you not look in the mirror and say negative things about yourself? _____

_____

_____

_____.

7. Read Ruth 1:22-2:1-3,8-10; Ruth 2:14-16

    a. According to Ruth 2:10, when Ruth went to glean in the field
        belonging to a man named Boaz, why did he notice her, when
        she was a foreigner? _____

        _____.

    b. According to Ruth 2:14-16, what did Boaz do for Ruth
        because of his attitude toward her?_____

        _____

        _____

        _____

        _____

        _____.

    c. What happened because of the favor that Ruth found in the
        eyes of Boaz?_____

        _____

        _____

        _____.

    d. That is a marvelous example and picture of _____

        _____.

        How does it relate to us today? _____

        _____

        _____

        _____

        _____

_____
_____.

8. a. Although we cannot produce supernatural favor, because it is received as a gift from the Lord, what are we doing when we do all the things that produce natural favor — being kind to others, treating people with respect and dignity, edifying and building up others? _____
_____.

  b. As we treat people right and look to God to give us favor, we are _____
_____.

9. a. It is often said of those who enjoy special favor with God or with men that they are "favored." What does it mean to be favored? _____
_____.

  b. Is it pride for us to want to be featured? _____
_____
_____
_____
_____
_____.

  c. What does God do to feature a person? _____
_____
_____
_____
_____.

d. To whom does this happen? _____

_____

_____

_____

_____.

e. Why does God want to give us supernatural favor? _____

_____

_____.

f. There are so many things that God would love to do for us, but He cannot because _____.

g. Why don't we ask God to do for us what He wants to do?_____

_____.

h. When is the only time we will go to God and ask for special favor?_____

_____

_____

_____.

i. When we do something nice for someone else, we are sowing the seed for God to_____

_____.

j. To be favored or featured is to _____

_____

_____.

10. a. What does it mean to be a favorite? _____

_____

_____
_____
_____
_____
_____.

b. If there is nothing about us that can cause us to become God's
    favorite, how can we occupy that place of honor and esteem?

    _____
    _____
    _____
    _____.

c. Why is God able to say to every single one of us at the same
    time, and sincerely mean it, "You are the apple of My eye; you
    are My favorite child"? _____
    _____
    _____
    _____.

d. Why does God assure each of us that we are His favorite
    child? _____
    _____
    _____
    _____
    _____
    _____.

11. Read Psalm 8:1-6; 1 Corinthians 2:14 KJV; Exodus 34:28-35

a. What does verse 5 of Psalm 8 tell us that God has done for man? _____
_____.

b. In this context, what three words have special significance?
_____
_____.

c. In the author's opinion, which two words here have the same meaning? _____.

d. Based on Psalm 8:1-6, what example does she give to illustrate her opinion?_____
_____
_____
_____
_____.

e. How does the author describe the word "glory" in this instance? _____.

f. So what is the psalmist telling us in this passage?_____
_____
_____
_____.

g. What is the main reason we are not tapping into the blessings of the Lord which have been placed upon us?_____
_____
_____

_____
_____.

h. According to verse 6 of Psalm 8, why are we not supposed to allow the devil and his demons to intimidate, dominate and oppress us? _____

_____
_____
_____.

i. What is another way the author describes the word "glory"?

_____
_____.

j. The author says she has seen the word "honor" described as

_____
_____.

k. What then will happen to us if we will walk in the blessings of glory and honor with which the Lord our God has crowned us? _____

_____
_____
_____
_____
_____.

12. a. When we spend time soaking up the presence of the Lord, no one can see it on us_____,
but they can sense it _____.

b. What is the reason they may find themselves drawn to us without even knowing or understanding why? _____ _____ _____.

c. There is a _____ that goes with spending time in communion with our heavenly Father.

d. If you have ever found yourself enjoying supernatural favor with people, it is because _____ _____.

e. When that happens to us, all we can do is _____ _____.

13.   Read John 17:22; review Luke 2:52

a. What did we read about Jesus in Luke 2:52? _____ _____ _____.

b. In John 17:22, as Jesus is praying to His Father just before His departure into heaven, what does Jesus say that He has given to us His disciples? Why? _____ _____ _____ _____.

c. What then should we be believing and confessing? _____ _____ _____ _____.

d. For what should we be praising and thanking God?_____

_____

_____

_____

_____

_____.

14. Read 2 Corinthians 5:18-20; 1 Peter 2:11; Revelation 1:6 KJV

a. What should we understand by the passage in 2 Corinthians 5:18-20? _____

_____

_____.

b. Why then do we not have God's favor? _____

_____

_____.

c. Why did Jesus come? _____

_____

_____.

d. It is part of our _____ to have and enjoy favor. It is part of our _____ to act as Christ's ambassadors by drawing others to receive God's wonderful gift of forgiveness and reconciliation and to share in His marvelous grace, His _____.

e. God wants to restore us to favor with Himself so that we may act as His _____ in the earth. That is how we need to look upon ourselves, as _____ _____from a foreign land.

f. As foreign ambassadors, how should we expect to be treated and how should we treat others to whom we are sent by the Lord for the sake of His Kingdom? _____

_____ .

g. In Revelation 1:6 KJV, the Bible tells us that not only are we ambassadors for Christ, but that we are _____ _____ and_____ unto our God. That is why we need a different attitude toward ourselves and others. We need to be acting like _____ _____, like

_____ .

15. Read Ephesians 6:11,12; 2 Timothy 1:7

a. The passage in Ephesians 6:11,12 indicates that we are in a spiritual war. Whether we use the word "militantly" or the word "aggressively" to describe how believers need to walk through life, we are saying the same thing: we believers need to be confident and assured, not _____ and _____. We need to know _____

_____

_____

_____ .

b. That doesn't mean we should have a bad attitude or be pushy or overbearing toward others. This is how we are to act toward the evil spirits who oppose and harass us. We should be behaving in the _____ realm the way the Bible says we are in the _____

_____ realm.

c. If people have a bad attitude toward you, it may be because you are not walking in the _____ _____.

It may be because you are abdicating your _____ _____.

It may be because you are bowing down to demonic spirits, giving them the _____ _____.

16. Read Numbers 13:1,2,25-28,30-33; 1 Corinthians 1:30

a. When the Children of Israel drew near to their destination and Moses sent twelve men on a scouting expedition into the land of Canaan, what kind of report did ten of the twelve give when they returned? _____.

b. What kind of report did only two of them, Joshua and Caleb, give? _____.

c. What was the difference in the way these two groups looked at the situation? _____ _____ _____ _____ _____.

d. In verse 33 of Numbers chapter 13, what did the ten say of the inhabitants of the land and of themselves? _____ _____ _____

_____
_____
_____
_____.

e. How do you see yourself, as a grasshopper or as a mighty war-
    rior of God? Is yours an evil report or a good report? _____
    _____
    _____.

f. Ten of the Israelites saw _____
    . . . two saw _____!

g. Keep your eyes on _____. You plus
    _____ is enough in any situation.

h. God can cause you to be accepted. He can put you over. He
    can give you the courage and the confidence you need to be
    a winner. But what three things must you do?_____
    _____
    _____
    _____
    _____
    _____.

i. Not only must you learn to see yourself differently, but also
    to _____ yourself differently.

j. Spiritually, Jesus died to lift you up and set you with Him in
    heavenly places. No matter how lowly you were before, you

now have _____

_____.

k. No matter how you may have dressed before, now you have on a robe of righteousness with a signet ring upon your finger. What does that signet ring mean? _____

_____

_____.

l. Based on 1 Corinthians 1:30, you need to stop seeing yourself as an unworthy sinner and begin to see yourself as ____

_____

_____.

17. Read 1 Corinthians 1:27-29; 1 Samuel 2:7

a. We have it backwards. We think God is looking for people who have "got it all together." But that is not true. Based on 1 Corinthians 1:27-29, He is looking for those who _____

_____

_____.

b. If we will be careful not to get haughty or arrogant, the Lord can use us mightily. But the minute we get lifted up in pride, He will be obligated to bring us down. What must we remember from 1 Samuel 2:7? _____

_____

_____.

c. The goal is to keep what in mind? _____

_____

_____

_____

_____.

18. Read 2 Corinthians 5:20

    a. Based on this verse, who are we?_____

       _____

       _____

       _____.

    b. What does that mean? _____

       _____

       _____

       _____

       _____

       _____.

    c. What does Jesus do through us, His personal representatives on this earth? _____

       _____

       _____

       _____

       _____.

    d. What is Paul saying to us in this verse? _____

       _____

       _____

       _____

       _____

       _____.

19. Read Numbers 6:22-26; Numbers 6:25,26 KJV; Matthew 5:16 KJV; Galatians 6:7 KJV

    a. Based on Numbers 6:22-26, what is God's countenance? _____
       _____.

    b. When any man or woman of God says to us, "The Lord make his face shine upon thee, and be gracious unto thee: The Lord lift up his countenance upon thee, and give thee peace," what is he or she saying? _____
       _____
       _____
       _____.

    c. Letting your light shine can be as simple as _____
       _____. That is one way to "flip on the switch" of _____
       _____.

    d. Show favor as often as you can to as many as you can. By so doing, you will _____
       _____.

20. Read Genesis 12:2

    a. In closing this chapter, what does the author encourage you to do?_____
       _____
       _____
       _____.

b. In Genesis 12:2, what did God tell Abraham? _____
    _____.

c. If you pray for favor in a certain place and it does not work, why should you not get discouraged? _____
    _____
    _____
    _____.

d. What should you do when you find yourself in a situation in which things are not turning out as you would like? _____
    _____
    _____
    _____.

e. What will happen if everywhere you go you pray for divine favor upon all concerned — upon others and upon yourself?
    _____
    _____.

An Attitude of Gratitude

1. a. What kind of a people does God desire and not desire? _____

    _____

    _____

    _____.

    b. Though we may call the negative attitude of the nation of Israel many names, God called it _____.

    c. What lesson do we need to learn just as much as the Children of Israel did? _____

    _____

    _____

    _____.

    d. What is one thing that will help us learn that lesson? _____

    _____.

2. Read Romans 4:4; Romans 4:2; 1 Corinthians 15:10

    a. What does Romans 4:4 imply? _____

    _____

    _____

    _____

    _____

    _____.

    b. There is nothing that can cause a person to become more haughty and proud than what he considers _____

    _____.

And there is nothing that can cause a person to overflow with gratitude and thanksgiving more than a _____ _____ _____.

c. If we think that whatever blessing we receive from God is proof of our own personal holiness and righteousness, what kind of attitude are we going to have and what will be the result of it? _____ _____ _____ _____ _____.

d. What do we in the Body of Christ often think to ourselves when we look at those who are having a hard time?_____ _____ _____ _____.

e. What must we remember that the Apostle Paul said about himself in 1 Corinthians 15:10? _____ _____.

3. a. When we talk about the Holy Spirit, we are talking about____ _____, which is _____ _____ _____ _____.

b. We will never be the kind of thankful, grateful people God desires us to be until we recognize the truth that _____ _____ _____.

c. As human beings, even we Christians are subject to _____ _____ and _____.

d. Although as the children of God, "as King's kids," we do have rights and an inheritance, we must also have a _____ _____. Without it, we will be_____ and _____.

e. Although we have multitudinous opportunities to complain on a regular basis, why should we not do so? _____ _____ _____ _____ _____.

f. How should we respond to the help we are already getting but don't deserve? _____ _____.

g. This is not just an occasional word of thanks, but a _____ _____ _____ _____.

4. Read John 11:41; 1 John 5:14,15; Psalm 26:7; Jonah 2:9; Matthew 11:25; Matthew 15:36; John 6:11; Mark 14:22,23

a. How does the author encourage you to end your prayer as Jesus did in John 11:41? _____ _____.

b. Based on 1 John 5:14,15, why does she encourage you to do that? _____ _____ _____.

c. According to Psalm 26:7 and Jonah 2:9, how do we overcome doubt? _____ _____.

d. Why is part of the power of prayer the power of thanksgiving? _____ _____.

e. During His earthly ministry, what kind of life did Jesus live? _____.

f. When and for what did He give thanks to the Father? _____ _____.

5. Read Philippians 4:6; Ephesians 5:20; 1 Thessalonians 5:18

a. In Philippians 4:6 Paul tells us how to live free from worry and anxiety — _____ _____.

b. When we come to God in prayer, asking Him to meet our current need, for what does He want us to be thankful? _____ _____.

c. What He desires is not so much an _____ of thanksgiving, but an _____ of thanksgiving.

d. In our prayers to God, our _____ and _____ should be more generous than our _____.

e. This kind of lifestyle of thanksgiving is evidence of a _____ _____, which is an indication that that individual is_____ _____.

f. In Philippians 4:6 Paul is not giving us a formula for getting what we want from God by constantly thanking Him for it. What he is presenting to us is a lifestyle of thanksgiving, an attitude of gratitude that gives thanks to God not only for _____ but also simply for _____.

6. Read 2 Corinthians 9:14,15; 2 Corinthians 2:14

a. Although, like Jesus, Paul gave thanks to God for many things, the thing he probably gave thanks for most, besides Christ Himself, was _____. Why? _____ _____ _____.

b. What is the problem with having all kinds of things to be thankful for in this life? _____

_____

_____.

c. Why do we do that? _____

_____.

d. If we are going to have an attitude of gratitude, we are going to have to do it _____.

7. Read Zechariah 12:1-3,8-10

a. In this passage, what is God saying to His people? _____

_____

_____

_____

_____

_____.

b. There is no way to live in victory without an understanding of the Spirit of _____

and _____.

c. Why do these two words go together? _____

_____

_____

_____

_____.

d. Why is the message of grace such good news? _____

_____

_____.

e. We don't have to be perfect in order to get God to help us. All
we have to do to receive the help we need is to _____

_____

_____.

8. Read Hebrews 4:15,16

Isn't it wonderful that we don't have to _____

_____, constantly struggling,
striving and straining to reach and maintain _____
_____ without which we cannot feel assured
that God will answer our prayers and be gracious to us? Isn't it
great that we can come fearlessly and confidently and boldly to
God's_____

_____

_____ and receive mercy and
grace to help us in our time of need?

9. Read James 4:1,2

a. Based on this passage, why are we miserable and unhappy, frustrated, unable to get along with each other, always so upset and
in constant turmoil and not walking in joy and peace? _____

_____

_____.

b. Even though we are born again and baptized in the Holy
Spirit, what is one of the most important things we must learn

and apply in our life if we are to live victoriously?_____

_____

_____.

c. What does the Bible promise us will happen whenever we try to accomplish something on our own?_____

_____

_____

_____

_____

_____

_____.

d. Why must we be totally dependent upon the Lord, not merely trying to use "casting and asking" as a form of manipulation in order to get what we want out of either God or other people? _____

_____

_____.

e. What is the only way to find real peace and joy in life? _____

_____

_____

_____

_____.

10. Read Luke 11:9-13; Matthew 7:7-11; review James 4:2 KJV; review John 16:24 KJV

    a. Who is the Spirit of grace and supplication? _____

    _____. How is this gift

from God received? _____
_____.

b. What do both Luke 11:9-13 and Matthew 7:7-11 tell us? _____

_____
_____
_____
_____
_____.

c. When we try to get healed, try to be prosperous and try to handle our own problems without asking God to work them out for us, what is our mistake? _____

_____
_____
_____
_____.

d. What is the important difference between what Jesus says in Matthew 7:11 and what He says in Luke 11:13? _____

_____
_____
_____
_____
_____.

e. What is the most important of the "good things" that God wants to give us? _____.

f. What is the Holy Spirit given to us for? _____

_____

_____.

g. Instead of trying so hard to make things happen to meet our own needs, if we need something, all we have to do is_____

_____.

h. What did Jesus mean when He said to His disciples that it was better or more advantageous for them if He left them?_____

_____

_____

_____

_____

_____.

11. Read John 14:16,17

a. Who is the Holy Spirit, and how does this Spirit come to live within us? _____

_____

_____

_____

_____

_____.

b. Based on John 14:16,17, what is the Holy Spirit's multiple role?_____

_____

_____.

    c. What is the purpose of the Holy Spirit? _____

_____

_____

_____.

12.   Read Romans 15:15,16 KJV; John 14:2 KJV

    a. In John 14:2 KJV Jesus told His disciples that He was going to prepare a place for them. Later in that same chapter He told them that He would ask the Father to give them another Comforter, the Holy Spirit, to abide with them always. So just as Jesus has gone to prepare a place for us, He has sent the Holy Spirit to _____

_____.

    b. Based on Romans 15:16, Who is the Holy Spirit in our lives?

_____

_____.

    c. Why is there no such thing as a person becoming holy apart from a great involvement with the Holy Spirit in his life? _____

_____

_____

_____

_____.

13.   a. The word "Comforter," used to refer to the Holy Spirit, can be translated many ways according to the many roles or functions He plays in the life of the believer. What is one of those roles or functions? _____

_____.

b. Have you ever thought of the Holy Spirit, the Third Person of the Godhead, as your personal Helper? Have you ever asked for His help? _____.

c. Is it true or false that we believers can only call upon God for His help when we get into a situation that is far over our head, that He is only interested in getting involved in our lives when we face huge, desperate problems that fit into His divine category? _____ _____.

d. Why doesn't God just help us when He sees we need it? _____ _____ _____ _____ _____ _____ _____.

14. Read Psalm 121:2; Isaiah 40:31

a. What does the word "standby" mean to us in our modern jet age? _____ _____ _____.

b. How does this apply to the Holy Spirit as our Standby? _____ _____ _____ _____ _____

_____
_____.

c. One of the most spiritual prayers we can offer is the one-word prayer, _____!

d. As long as we keep trying to do everything ourselves in our own way and in our own strength, we not only frustrate ourselves, we also frustrate the grace of the Holy Spirit. Why? _____

_____
_____
_____
_____.

e. Why does much of our frustration in life come? _____

_____
_____
_____.

f. How can we avoid frustration? _____

_____
_____.

g. In Psalm 121:2 and Isaiah 40:31, what does the Lord promise those who wait upon Him? _____

_____.

h. Standing by to provide help and strength is just one of the roles and functions of the Holy Spirit. What is another? _____

_____
_____.

15. Read John 14:26; John 16:13 KJV

    a. According to John 14:26, Jesus said the Holy Spirit, Whom the Father sent in His name and in His place, was sent for what purpose?_____

    _____

    _____

    _____.

    b. Does that mean that we should never seek counsel or advice from others, especially those who are trained in this area? If not, what does it mean? _____

    _____

    _____

    _____.

    c. We believers must remember that_____ is our Counselor. If we don't know how to do something or how to handle some situation, we should simply say,_____

    _____.

    d. When you surrender a situation to the Lord, what should you do? Why? _____

    _____

    _____

    _____.

    e. According to John 16:13 KJV, what should you let the Counselor, the Spirit of Truth, do that He has been given to you to do? _____.

16.   Read John 14:27; Matthew 10:19,20

   a. In John 14:27, what does Jesus say He gives us and bequeaths
       to us? _____.

   b. Why can we not live in peace in this world if we don't know
       how to receive on a continual basis the ministry of the Holy
       Spirit? _____
       _____.

   c. If we want to live in peace, what must we do? _____
       _____
       _____
       _____
       _____
       _____
       _____.

   d. Based on John 14:27, instead of wearing ourselves out trying
       to prepare ourselves for every situation we are likely to run
       into in the future and planning and rehearsing every word we
       are going to speak in every interview and conversation, what
       is Jesus telling us to do? _____
       _____.

   e. If we will listen to what the Lord is telling us in John 14:27,
       not only will we have more peace, but we will also _____
       _____.

   f. The way we learn to trust the Holy Spirit is by getting to
       know Him, which comes from _____
       with Him.

17. Read John 16:7-11

     a. According to what Jesus tells us in John 16:7, why is the Holy
         Spirit given to us?_____
         _____
         _____.

     b. In regard to the Holy Spirit, what two things does the author
         encourage you to do? First,_____
         _____
         _____
         _____
         _____
         _____
         _____
         _____
         _____
         _____.

         Second, _____
         _____
         _____.

     c. How does the author suggest that you pray to the Lord on
         this subject?_____
         _____
         _____
         _____
         _____
         _____

_____
_____.

18. Read Ephesians 3:20,21; John 16:24

    a. The author says that Ephesians 3:20,21 sum up the whole message that she is presenting in this book. What is it?_____
    _____
    _____.

    b. God is able to do much more than we even know how to ask Him for. That is another reason why He gives us His Holy Spirit _____
    _____
    _____.

    c. How do you open the channel for God to begin to move in your life in a mighty way? _____
    _____.

    d. According to John 16:24, what should you do? Why? _____
    _____
    _____
    _____.

19. Read James 1:2-7; Hebrews 11:6; James 1:5 KJV

    a. What does James talk about in this passage? _____
    _____
    _____
    _____.

b. What does he tell us such things do for us? _____
    _____
    _____.

c. What then does he say that we are to do about them? Why?
    _____
    _____
    _____.

d. What is the first important point James gives in this passage
    when he says what we should do if we are deficient in wis-
    dom, if we don't know what to do in the midst of trials and
    temptations? _____
    _____.

e. What is the second important point James gives of who we
    are to ask? Why?_____
    _____
    _____.

f. What is the third important point James gives of how we are
    to ask? Why?_____
    _____.

g. What is the fourth important point James gives of the way we
    are to ask? _____
    _____
    _____
    _____.

h. According to James, God is what kind of a God? _____
    _____.

How does He give? _____.

To whom does He give? _____.

What is His attitude in giving? _____
_____.

i. How could we paraphrase James 1:5 KJV? _____
_____
_____
_____
_____
_____
_____
_____.

j. God will never allow us to manifest total perfection in this life. Why? _____
_____
_____.

k. Does that mean that we shouldn't keep pressing toward the mark of perfection? If not, what does it mean? _____
_____
_____.

20. Read Hebrews 13:15

a. Thanksgiving, gratitude and praise are forerunners to a _____
_____.

b. What is *praise?* _____
    _____
    _____
    _____
    _____.

c. What will be the result if we will continue to ask God, if we
    will keep receiving His grace and power?_____
    _____
    _____
    _____
    _____.

d. As we see in Hebrews 13:15, what should we be doing con-
    stantly and at all times? _____
    _____
    _____
    _____
    _____
    _____.

Living a Holy Life by Grace

1. Read 1 Corinthians 15:10 KJV; Galatians 2:21 KJV; Romans 5:17 KJV

    a. In Galatians 2:21 KJV, what did Paul mean when he said that he did not frustrate the grace of God?_____
    _____
    _____
    _____.

    b. In 1 Corinthians 15:10 KJV, what does Paul say about him-self? What does he add to that statement? _____
    _____
    _____
    _____
    _____.

    c. What does the word *vain* mean and how does it relate to God's grace? _____
    _____
    _____
    _____.

    d. What is God's purpose in bestowing His grace upon us?_____
    _____
    _____
    _____.

    e. If grace is the power of the Holy Spirit to come into our life and overcome our evil tendencies, what should those of us who have received an "abundance of grace" be able to do? _____

_____

_____ .

2. Read 1 Peter 1:14-16; Romans 8:28

    a. From this passage in 1 Peter, what does God obviously expect
        His children to be? _____

        _____ .

    b. What does it mean to be holy? What is *holiness?*_____

        _____

        _____

        _____

        _____ .

    c. What is another word used in the Word of God to describe
        those of us who have put our faith in Jesus Christ as Savior
        and Lord? _____ .

    d. As such, what are we supposed to do? _____

        _____

        _____

        _____

        _____ .

3. a. Why is the Holy Spirit called by that name, and what is His
        purpose in taking up residence in us? _____

        _____

        _____

        _____ .

b. Why has God sent His Spirit (the Comforter, Counselor, Helper, Intercessor, Advocate, Strengthener, and Standby)?

_____

_____.

c. What is the process called through which the Holy Spirit makes us holy, or leads us into holiness? _____

_____

_____.

4. a. The word "sanctification" is found throughout the New Testament. To what does it refer? _____

_____

_____

_____

_____

_____.

b. In regard to holiness, what question must we ask ourselves?

_____

_____

_____

_____?

c. As believers we are not to be anxious about holiness or the process of sanctification, but we are to be _____
_____ about it. What are we to do regarding it? _____

_____

_____

_____
_____
_____
_____
_____.

d. While we are not to worry about holiness, we are also not to
    have a light attitude toward _____.

5. Read Romans 5:20; 6:15,16 KJV

    a. When we talk about grace, we must be careful not to think of
        it as a blanket that covers us and gives us _____
        _____.

    b. What was the confused reasoning of the early believers about
        Paul's teaching on grace and sin in Romans 6:15?_____
        _____
        _____
        _____
        _____
        _____!

    c. What did Paul have to write to these people in Romans 6:16
        to straighten them out about their wrong thinking? _____
        _____
        _____
        _____
        _____.

d. Like the believers in Paul's day, our problem is not just a mis-understanding of _____, it is also a misunderstanding of _____.

e. What is grace supposed to accomplish in us? _____
_____.

6. a. If we learn to receive the grace of God, what is the practical, positive result we should see in our life? _____
_____
_____.

b. What mistake do we make that was made by the early believers so that Paul had to rebuke them and correct their thinking?
_____
_____
_____
_____
_____.

c. What does God's grace teach us? _____
_____
_____.

d. God's grace is given to us to do more than give us the power to live, it is also given to us to _____
_____.

e. According to the author, why is the Holy Spirit given to us?
_____
_____.

7. Read 1 Peter 1:22; John 16:13; review 1 Peter 1:14-16.

    a. According to 1 Peter 1:22, how do we obey the Truth? _____
        _____ .

    b. How do we obey the Truth that the Holy Spirit, the Spirit of
        Truth, shows us?_____
        _____ .

    c. According to John 16:13, what is part of the Holy Spirit's job?
        _____ .

    d. Once the Holy Spirit shows us what we should stop doing
        and start doing, then we need to_____
        _____
        _____
        _____ .

    e. A message about holiness without a message about empow-
        erment simply produces pressure. Why?_____
        _____
        _____
        _____
        _____ .

    f. What is the key to the sanctification process, and how is it
        revealed to us? _____
        _____
        _____
        _____
        _____ .

8. Read Romans 12:1

   a. In this verse, what is Paul saying that we are to dedicate to God? _____

      _____

      _____

      _____

      _____

      _____.

   b. If we want the light of God's countenance to shine upon us, what must we do? _____

      _____.

   c. We are to dedicate _____ our members and faculties to God as a _____, holy, devoted, consecrated (sanctified) and pleasing to God, which is our reasonable, rational, intelligent _____ _____ and

      _____.

   d. We are to serve and worship God totally with our body and spirit, but in Romans 12:1 Paul says that we are to serve and worship Him with our_____ also.

   e. We have to make a rational, conscious choice to follow holiness. God's part is to give us His grace and Spirit, our part is to give Him _____.

   f. There is a real balance involved in distinguishing between _____ in the Lord and being _____ about the things of God.

g. God wants us to cast our _____, but not our _____.

h. True holiness is a combined effort between _____ and _____.

9. Read Haggai 2:11-13

   a. In this study, how have we defined *holiness?* _____
   _____.

   b. The same Greek word translated *holiness* is also translated *sanctification*, which the Greek dictionary says _____
   _____
   _____.

   What does that mean? _____
   _____
   _____
   _____
   _____
   _____
   _____.

   c. What does that mean to us? _____
   _____
   _____
   _____
   _____.

d. As we see in this passage from the Old Testament prophet Haggai, _____ is infectious, _____ is not.

10. Read Romans 14:1-4

a. In addition to the problem of misunderstanding sin and grace, what is another major reason why people fail to live a holy life? _____

_____

_____.

b. As we have seen, holiness is an _____ matter.

c. One of the worst mistakes we can make is to try to _____

_____

_____

_____.

d. Another very similar mistake we make is to try to _____

_____

_____

_____.

e. According to the author, why do our "works of the flesh," our trying to convince others of the changes that we feel are needed in their personalities, actions and choices, only make the problem worse? _____

_____

_____.

f. Only _____ can change a human heart.
    When there is a change in our behavior, where does that
    change come from? _____
    _____.

g. In regard to personal convictions, what must you be on your
    guard against? Why? _____
    _____
    _____
    _____
    _____
    _____
    _____
    _____
    _____.

h. What is the problem for so many believers in this area? _____
    _____
    _____
    _____
    _____
    _____
    _____
    _____
    _____.

i. Our problem is that we are constantly trying to straighten out
    everybody else instead of _____
    _____

_____
_____
_____
_____!

j. Explain what is meant by the author's statement that holiness
    is an individual matter. _____

    _____
    _____
    _____
    _____
    _____.

k. What will happen if we become more involved in someone
    else's sanctification process than we are in our own? _____

    _____.

l. Instead of becoming so concerned with what others are doing
    or not doing that we fail to listen to the voice of the Holy
    Spirit Who is dealing with us about our own life, what should
    we do? _____

    _____
    _____
    _____.

11. Read Romans 14:10-13

    a. According to this passage, what is each of us going to do
        when we appear before God the Father? _____

        _____.

b. What then do we need to learn to do? _____

_____

_____

_____

_____ .

c. Based on this passage, since we will never all believe exactly
alike on everything, what are we told to do? _____

_____

_____ .

12. Read Romans 14:22,23; Romans 12:3

a. What does Romans 14:22,23 tell us?_____

_____

_____

_____ .

b. What does the author tell us about trying to cram our convictions down everybody else's throat? _____

_____ .

c. When we try to excuse ourselves or justify our actions in this
area by saying that we are just trying to help, what do we
need to remember?_____

_____

_____ .

d. When we have an impulse to try to help someone, what do
we have to be sure of before we take action? _____

_____ .

e. In Romans 12:3, what was Paul's warning to the Romans?_____

_____

_____

_____

_____.

f. Paul was humble enough to know that he had to warn or correct the Romans by _____ —
not by _____.

g. Verse 23 of Romans 14 tells us that the person who does
something against his conscience (perhaps because of us!)
stands condemned before God. Why? _____

_____

_____

_____.

h. What does it mean that whatever is not of faith is sin? _____

_____

_____

_____.

i. Why must we be constantly on our guard against trying to
put our convictions off on someone else? _____

_____

_____

_____

_____

_____.

13. Read 2 Corinthians 3:18; Deuteronomy 7:22

   a. What does Paul say to us in 2 Corinthians 3:18? _____

   _____

   _____

   _____ .

   b. What does that mean? _____

   _____ .

   c. Legally and positionally, we are Holy in Christ. But experien-
   tially, the holiness is being manifested through us in degrees
   of glory that are progressive. That is what we have called the

   _____

   _____ , part of which is

   _____

   _____

   _____ .

   d. Although we are to pursue holiness "earnestly and undeviat-
   ingly," although we are to desire it fully and cooperate in it,
   holiness, "or sanctification, is not an attainment, it is the

   _____

   _____ .

   e. Just as the Children of Israel were delivered from their enemies in Deuteronomy 7:22, how are we delivered out of our
   sins? _____ .

   f. How does God say we must proceed from sinfulness to holiness? _____ .

g. There is no way to travel from the state of sinfulness to the state of holiness except _____ _____.

14. Read Philippians 2:12; Galatians 3:16; 1 Corinthians 3:6; Ephesians 5:26; Matthew 12:34 KJV; 2 Peter 3:18

   a. What is the basic message of Philippians 2:12 as set forth clearly and simply in the last part of the *King James Version?* _____ _____.

   b. Jesus is the Seed spoken of in Galatians 3:16. Based on this Scripture, when Paul tells us to work out our own salvation with fear and trembling, what does he mean? _____ _____ _____ _____ _____.

   c. Based on 1 Corinthians 3:6 and Ephesians 5:26, how do we water the seed of holiness in us? _____ _____.

   d. What happens as we water the seed of holiness in us? _____ _____ _____ _____.

   e. What does 2 Peter 3:18 mean when it speaks of growing in the grace and knowledge of our Lord Jesus Christ? _____ _____.

f. What should you do if you have not arrived at your destination — if you have not reached your goal? _____

_____

_____

_____.

15. Read Philippians 2:13

a. How is this process of sanctification carried out? How is the growth in grace accomplished? _____

_____

_____

_____

_____

_____.

b. How does the process of sanctification work? _____

_____

_____

_____

_____

_____

_____.

16. Read James 1:21,22; Isaiah 64:6

a. The Holy Spirit is one agent of the process of sanctification, but what is the other agent? _____

_____.

b. It is our job to hear the Word and be doers of the Word, but it is not our job to work the Word. Who causes the Word to work within us?_____.

c. For what reason does the author believe that despite hearing the Word, we are still not changing as we should? _____
_____
_____.

d. Not only must we hear the Word, we must also_____
_____
_____
_____.

e. Why do we need to receive and welcome the Word of God with meekness?_____
_____.

f. What is the only way to be truly refined and purified?_____
_____
_____
_____
_____
_____
_____
_____.

17. Read Malachi 3:1-3; Matthew 3:11

a. In the Old Testament prophecy in Malachi 3:1-3, what is Jesus, the Messiah, said to be like? _____
_____.

b. Later, in the New Testament we read about the Holy Spirit being like _____.

c. We have heard a lot about the Holy Spirit being like fire, but we have never heard much about His being like _____ _____.

18. Read John 16:7,8; John 17:17-19; Ephesians 5:25-27

a. In John 16:7,8 Jesus speaks to His disciples about the various roles and functions of the Holy Spirit, one of which is to _____ _____.

b. Later on in John 17:17-19 we begin to see the Holy Spirit in another light, as the One Who _____ _____ _____.

c. Based on the passage in Ephesians 5:25-27, we see that the Holy Spirit is like fullers' soap, and the Word of God is like water. If so, how are we sanctified?_____ _____ _____.

d. What do we do wrong in regard to the things of God?_____ _____ _____ _____ _____ _____ _____.

e.   What do we do if the stains of sin are so set in that one application of soap and water doesn't seem to be enough? How do we remove stubborn stains left by sin? What is needed?

_____

_____

_____

_____.

19.   Read 1 Peter 5:10,11; Romans 3:23 KJV; Hebrews 6:12 KJV; Romans 5:20; 2 Corinthians 12:9

a.   What kind of process do you go through to find peace with God and yourself once you have sinned? _____

_____

_____.

b.   When the author sins, instead of applying a generous amount of God's powerful grace, what does she say she usually tries?

_____

_____

_____.

c.   What one good thing has come out of her process of dealing with sin in her life? _____

_____!

d.   In essence, what does she do after she has messed up things all the way around? _____

_____

_____

_____

_____
_____
_____
_____
_____.

e. According to Hebrews 6:12 KJV, how do we receive the prom-
    ises of God? _____.

f. Why must we suffer at all? Many times why does suffering
    come? _____
    _____
    _____
    _____
    _____
    _____
    _____
    _____
    _____.

g. According to Romans 5:20, what is the answer to sin?_____
    _____.

h. The struggling of fleshly effort won't deliver anyone, but
    God's grace never fails us. If you have big problems, what
    should you remember?_____
    _____
    _____.

i. God does not just offer us grace, but He offers us_____
    _____.

Conclusion

1. Why does the author say that the message on grace has been the single most important message that the Holy Spirit has ministered to her? _____

    _____.

2. How does she sometimes refer to grace?_____

    _____.

3. Why does she pray that you will read *If Not for the Grace of God* several times over the years? _____

    _____

    _____

    _____

    _____

    _____.

4. What two things does she want you to remember?_____

    _____

    _____

    _____

    _____

    _____.

5. The grace of God makes _____ the task that would have been _____ or even _____.

6. Read Matthew 11:28-30

    a. Although the devil wants to place heavy burdens upon our
        shoulders — the burdens of works of the flesh, the burden of
        the law and fleshly effort to keep it — what has Jesus prom-
        ised us in this passage? _____

        _____.

    b. Don't be satisfied with just enough grace to save you from
        eternal damnation. Receive not only that grace which saves,
        but receive_____

        _____ so you may

        live victoriously and glorify Jesus in your daily life.

Prayer for a
Personal Relationship
With the Lord

God wants you to receive His free gift of salvation. Jesus wants to save you and fill you with the Holy Spirit more than anything. If you have never invited Jesus, the Prince of Peace, to be your Lord and Savior, I invite you to do so now. Pray the following prayer, and if you are really sincere about it, you will experience a new life in Christ.

Father,

You loved the world so much, You gave Your only begotten Son to die for our sins so that whoever believes in Him will not perish, but have eternal life.

Your Word says we are saved by grace through faith as a gift from You. There is nothing we can do to earn salvation.

I believe and confess with my mouth that Jesus Christ is Your Son, the Savior of the world. I believe He died on the cross for me and bore all of my sins, paying the price for them. I believe in my heart that You raised Jesus from the dead.

I ask You to forgive my sins. I confess Jesus as my Lord. According to Your Word, I am saved and will spend eternity with You! Thank You, Father. I am so grateful! In Jesus' name, amen.

See John 3:16; Ephesians 2:8,9; Romans 10:9,10; 1 Corinthians 15:3,4; 1 John 1:9; 4:14-16; 5:1,12,13.

Answers

Introduction

1. The power of God available to meet our needs without any cost to us.

2. By believing rather than through human effort.

3. A clear understanding of grace.

4a. Everything in the Bible — salvation, the infilling of the Holy Spirit, fellowship with God and all victory in our daily lives.

4b. We are nothing, we have nothing, we can do nothing.

4c. We would all be miserable and hopeless.

5a. He ". . . grew and became strong in spirit, filled with wisdom; and the grace (favor and spiritual blessing) of God was upon Him."

5b. The same thing that Jesus needed: we need to become strong in spirit, filled with God's wisdom and having His grace upon us.

5c. Nothing will be impossible to us. Nothing is possible to us.

5d. By the grace of God.

6a. Paul tells us that we are God's handiwork, His workmanship, and that we are recreated in Christ Jesus so that we can do all the good works, follow all the paths and live the good life that God has planned and arranged for us.

6b. That our works were prepared for us by God ". . . from the foundation of the world."

6c. Because God chose us and laid out our life work for us before we were ever born, before the world was even created.

6d. That apart from Him we can do nothing.

6e. It means that we are partners with God. He allows us to share in His glory as long as we remember that apart from Him we can do nothing.

6f. None of the things that go wrong will upset or discourage us. Because we will know that through it all God is working out His plan for us. We will not glory in what we are doing for God, but only in what He is doing through us.

6g. Divine willingness to use His infinite power to meet our needs — and at no cost to us whatsoever.

6h. Cast them upon the Lord. Make a commitment to put all that aside for a moment. Free yourself from all attempts to achieve anything by your own faith and effort. Instead, just relax and place your trust solely upon the Lord. Let go completely and see what dynamic power He will bring to bear in your life as you simply yield yourself to receive His amazing grace. You will see such a change in your entire approach to life that you will never desire to return to old ways.

Chapter 1

1a. We try to work the Word rather than let the Word work in us.

1b. Beat us over the head with it as condemnation.

1c. Something you can't do anything about.

2a. Because the Law has the ability to do one of two things: If we follow it perfectly, it can make us holy. But since no human being can do that, the second thing the Law can do is to actually increase sin, which leads to destruction.

2b. He gave it so man would try to keep it, find out he could not, and realize his desperate need for a savior.

2c. To disappoint, to prevent from obtaining a goal or fulfilling a desire.[1]

2d. Frustration.

3a. It is used in the sense of putting someone or something to the test.

3b. It refers to a test or trial to determine the value and worth of a person or thing.

3c. We use it in referring to human effort.

3d. Attempting to achieve or accomplish something by our own means or ability.

3e. Attempt anything without asking for God's help. We lean on Him the whole way through each project. We maintain an attitude that says, "Apart from Him I can do nothing."

3f. Exchange trying for trusting.

4a. Sensual desires that are ever warring in our bodily members.

4b. The nature of the Kingdom of God — and Jesus has told us that the Kingdom is within us.

4c. Righteousness, peace; joy. Heritage; inheritance.

4d. By trying to get it in the wrong way.

5a. As hatred.

5b. It says that to hate others because of their special gifts is to become a murderer in the heart.

5c. Stops trying to do it on his own and starts allowing the Lord to bring it to pass in His own way and in His own time.

5d. Because we do not ask.

5e. Ask, that we may receive that our joy may be full. Because the flesh, our carnal human nature, wants to do things itself.

5f. Because we are trying to obtain by our efforts what God wants to give us by His grace.

5g. We must be humble enough to quit trying and start trusting. We must be willing to stop doing and start asking.

6a. "Get." "Receive."

6b. Because we ask with the wrong motive or intention.

6c. He still has some work to do in us to prepare us for it.

6d. It helps us get truly rooted and grounded in Him. Our motives are wrong.

6e. We are not yet ready to receive it.

6f. He has something better in mind and we just don't know enough to ask Him for it, so He has to make us wait until we catch up with His plan, or we are out of His timing.

6g. God's grace.

7. Trying to do everything on our own or running to others with our problems rather than running to God.

8a. "Undeserved favor."

8b. The power of the Holy Spirit to meet the evil tendency within each of us.

8c. The evil tendency to be like an unfaithful wife, the evil tendency to have illicit love affairs with the world, the evil tendency to turn away from God and look to ourselves or to others rather than simply asking Him to meet our needs.

8d. It is a tendency of the flesh, and it is not the way God wants us to react.

8e. In the midst of all our problems and frustrations God gives us more and more grace, more and more power of the Holy Spirit to meet this evil tendency and all others fully.

9a. By grace through faith.

9b. We enter God's rest.

9c. Because instead of exercising faith in God, we are actually exercising faith in faith. We are worshipping a thing (faith) rather than worshipping a Person (God).

9d. God's blessings cannot be bought by faith or by anything else, they must be received. Faith is not the price that buys God's blessing, it is the hand that receives His blessing.

9e. The grace of God through our faith — that is, by believing (adhering to, trusting in and relying on) God, Who freely gives us all good things to enjoy.

9f. The same way we are saved, by grace through faith.

9g. Because we have all sinned and come short of the glory of God.

9h. The mistake of turning from living by grace to living by works.

10a. Works; grace.

10b. Faith is the channel through which we receive the grace of God to meet our needs.

10c. Grace is the power of God coming to us through our faith to meet our need.

10d. Frustration.

10e. Things to be a certain way, and in this life everything just does not always work out the way we want it to, the way we have planned for it to work.

10f. Trust Him enough to allow Him to do so.

11a. Proud; humble.

11b. Pride; obedient.

11c. It is the difference between pride and humility, between frustration and rest.

11d. Because *The Amplified Bible* version of 1 Peter 5:5 tells us that God opposes, frustrates, and defeats the proud, the insolent, the overbearing, the disdainful, the presumptuous, the boastful.

11e. They are the ones who try to figure out everything for themselves, those who try to do it their way rather than God's way. They are the ones who try to change themselves into what they think they ought to be rather than asking God to bring about within them the changes that He desires to make.

11f. Because He knows that if He allows us to do things our way, we will never learn to lean on Him.

12. It means to ask the Lord for what you need and then wait on Him to provide it as He sees fit, knowing that His timing is always perfect. It means to be still and know that He is God, and that He knows what is best for you in every situation of life. It means to stop trying to make things happen yourself and to allow the Lord to show you what you need to do to cooperate with His plan and purpose for you.

13a. Because worry is a work of the flesh. It is trying to figure out what to do to save oneself rather than trusting in God for deliverance.

13b. All traces of anxiety.

13c. You will not fulfill the works of the flesh.

14a. While we are waiting on the Lord, we must remain steadfast against the devil, our enemy who is out to devour us.

14b. He exhorts us to be firm in faith, rooted, established, strong, immovable and determined as we stand our ground in faith and trust, leaning not on our own strength but on the strength and power of the Lord.

15a. Faith is the leaning of the entire human personality on God in absolute trust and confidence in His power, wisdom and goodness.

15b. 1) His power and ability to do what needs to be done, 2) His wisdom and knowledge to do it when it needs to be done, and 3) His goodness and love to do it the way it needs to be done.

15c. (Your answer.)

15d. Letting go and letting God.

16a. ". . . trusted [Himself and everything] to Him Who judges fairly."

16b. Faith.

17a. The attitude of faith and trust in His Father that carried Him through the hard times He had to face.

17b. Our faith and trust in the Lord.

17c. It sustains us until God's power — in the form of grace — arrives on the scene to set us free.

17d. If we are not careful we can get our eyes fastened on the blessing rather than on the Lord.

17e. We must be very careful that we seek the Lord's face and not His hand. He wants us to seek Him, and not just what He can do for us.

17f. We begin to worship — adhere to, trust in and rely on — our faith rather than the Lord, the One on Whom our faith is based.

17g. We frustrate God's grace which is based not on our works but upon His unmerited favor toward us.

17h. We must learn to lean totally upon the Lord, freely acknowledging that it is not by faith but by grace that we receive any of the good things that He wants us to have. We must remember that the most important thing in receiving God's blessings is not our great faith but His great faithfulness.

18a. He told them that what they were witnessing that day was the direct result of God's faithfulness to keep His Word to raise up Jesus from the dead and to pour out His Spirit upon all mankind.

18b. He exercised faith and trust in His Father to do what He had promised He would do.

18c. He was not disappointed. His Spirit was not deserted in Hades nor was His body left to rot in the tomb. Instead, He was lifted up and made to sit at the right hand of God in the heavens from which He poured forth the promised Holy Spirit.

18d. You will not be deserted in your problem or left to rot in your dilemma.

18e. The grace of God.

19a. We get our eyes on faith, expecting it to do the work, but we fail to look beyond our faith to the source of power that causes it to work, which is the Lord.

19b. It kept Him stable until the Father's appointed time for His deliverance.

19c. By grace through faith.

19d. We will end up frustrated, trying to make things happen that we have no power to make happen.

19e. To get our eyes off our ability to believe and onto God's willingness to meet our need even though we do not have perfect faith.

19f. Jesus told him that all things are possible to those who believe.

19g. Jesus healed his son.

19h. Grace.

Chapter 2

1a. Mountain-moving grace.

1b. The Samaritans.

1c. It made them so angry that they began to do everything in their power to harass and cause trouble for the Israelites, to frustrate their purpose and plans.

1d. Because in these passages Jesus warned us that in this life we will have tribulation. He said that if people hated and persecuted Him, they will also hate and persecute us, because we belong to Him.

1e. It frustrates us and makes us miserable and unhappy.

1f. Their misunderstanding and frustration can cause them to give up and fall away.

1g. We try to use faith to get to the place where there is total freedom from trouble. It just doesn't work that way.

1h. The purpose of faith is not always to keep us from having trouble; it is often to carry us through trouble. If we never had any trouble, we wouldn't need any faith.

1i. Learning to be stable in hard times.

1j. Be prepared for a counterattack. It is not enough to win a victory, you have to be prepared to keep the victory you have won.

1k. Be constantly on the alert.

1l. Respond to the trouble caused by our enemy.

2a. He saw a lampstand made of gold with seven lamps upon it. There were seven pipes to the lamps on the stand and two olive trees, one on either side, to feed the lamps continuously with oil.

2b. The Holy Spirit.

2c. The power of Almighty God.

2d. Power of the Holy Spirit to meet our evil tendencies. It means that grace is the power of God to meet our needs and solve our problems.

3a. ". . . Not by might, nor by power, but by My Spirit [of Whom the oil is a symbol], says the Lord of hosts."

3b. He is telling them how they should react to their frustrating situation. He is saying to them that their response to trouble should be to depend not upon their own abilities or efforts, but upon the limitless power of the Holy Spirit to meet the issues and resolve the crises they face.

4a. A mountain of human obstacles, frustrating them and preventing them from doing what God had commanded them to do.

4b. Perspective. Many times we get so caught up in trying to deal with our enemy by our own strength and effort that we lose sight of our relationship with God.

4c. The enemy and his works; the Lord and His limitless power.

4d. We magnify the problem over the Problem-Solver.

4e. By doing what God is saying in Zechariah 4:7 and looking not at the problems, but at the Lord and His power.

4f. Complete your God-given task; grace — the power of the Holy Spirit.

4g. The Spirit.

4h. Faith; grace.

5a. The channel through which we receive the grace of God, which is the power of the Holy Spirit.

5b. Because like faith, they are mere channels through which we receive from God.

5c. That without faith it is impossible to please God.

5d. Because it is the means through which we receive from God all the good things He wants to provide us.

5e. He wants them to get their eyes on Him and learn to believe Him so He can do for and through them what He wants done in the earth.

5f. These things instead of the Lord Himself.

5g. Faith; God.

5h. Because there is such a fine line between the two.

5i. They are plugged into the divine power source.

6a. You are not plugged in.

6b. At peace within; the Spirit of the Lord.

6c. We should be saying, "Grace, grace to the mountain."

6d. Confusion.

6e. Personal relationship with God; time.

6f. God. Look beyond ways to eliminate our problems; the Lord in the midst of our problems.

6g. Because they do not allow for the individual differences in people.

6h. Personal fellowship with the Living God.

7a. God Himself.

7b. Fellowship with the Lord.

7c. ". . . be strong in the Lord, and in the power of his might."

7d. Those who are doing damage to his kingdom, those who are doing something for God.

7e. By girding on the full armor of God, taking up the shield of faith, by which we can quench all his fiery darts, and by wielding the sword of the Spirit, which is the Word of God.

7f. Spending time in fellowship with the Lord.

7g. After being strengthened in fellowship with God.

7h. Presence; power.

7i. Because each person is different and has to learn for himself how to communicate with his Creator.

7j. Because the Lord knows that you are facing a situation that is going to put a drain on your physical and spiritual resources.

7k. From God, not from methods.

7l. Come apart; come apart. Remain stable as you deal with the daily affairs of life.

8a. Unmerited favor; gift.

8b. "Buyable."

8c. Plugged into. Stay plugged in.

8d. The presence and power of the One Who lives His life in us and through us.

8e. Because we do too much and get all caught up in ourselves.

8f. We are not thankful and grateful because we think we earned the results by our own effort.

9a. A laborer receives wages, which are not considered a favor or a gift, but an obligation owed to him for his work. A believer receives God's gift of grace, which is based not on his efforts, but on his faith in God Who freely accepts him as righteous, the standing acceptable to God.

9b. It makes our fellowshipping with God become work rather than grace.

9c. To avoid falling into the trap of thinking that we deserve anything good from the Lord.

9d. To die and spend eternity in everlasting punishment. Because in the Lord's eyes, all of our righteousness, every good thing that we could ever do, is like filthy rags.

9e. We will see ourselves as we really are, knowing who we are in Christ Jesus, not in our own works or efforts.

9f. The fact that we love Him and want to be in His presence.

9g. It means that while people can sow seeds, they can't make them grow and produce a harvest.

9h. To a farmer who sows his seed in his field and then goes to sleep, and rises night and day, and the seed springs forth and grows up, ". . . he knoweth not how."

9i. Because His grace is a gift.

9j. Not by works but by grace, through faith.

10a. To have faith (constantly) in God — not in our faith or confession.

10b. We may think that it is our faith and our confession that make what we say come to pass.

10c. Put our trust in Him and not in our words or actions.

10d. Remains in Him, not our confession.

11a. That He is able — able to do far above and beyond anything that we can ever dare to hope, ask or even think.

11b. "According to [or by] the power [or grace of God] that worketh in us."

11c. The amount of grace we learn to receive.

11d. Because we are trying to do it apart from Him so we can take the credit and the glory that rightfully belong to Him.

11e. Every time something good comes into our life, instead of boasting and taking credit for it because of our great faith or confession or other works, we will automatically respond, "O God, thank You!"

12a. "Did you receive the Lord through your own works and efforts or by hearing the Gospel message and saying, 'I believe that?'"

12b. "Are you really so foolish and senseless and silly as to begin your new life by the Spirit and then try to reach perfection by depending on your own weak human flesh?"

12c. "Have you suffered all these things for nothing and to no purpose? Do you really want to go back now and start the sanctification process all over again?"

12d. "Does God supply your every need and work miracles among you because you keep the Law perfectly or because you put your entire faith and trust in the message you heard?"

12e. Ask the Lord to change us — and then leave it to Him.

12f. That He has to be our Source and our Supply.

12g. Bring about the many changes that need to be made in our life.

12h. We have done something to deserve it or earn it.

12i. Because you may not be willing to allow Him to bring about the change and to receive all the credit and the glory.

12j. Trying to do everything for ourselves.

13a. Not from ourselves, but from the Spirit of God as we continue to behold the glory of God.

13b. As we continue in His Word, He changes us.

13c. The credit is His, not ours.

14a. God.

14b. The truth that the work is the Lord's, not ours.

14c. We can enter His joy.

15a. To keep them off yourself and your troubles and instead to fasten them firmly on Jesus and His power.

15b. Because He already knows what is wrong with you. He is ready, willing and able to bring about the changes that need to be made in you and your life. He will bring you to maturity and perfection — if you will just ask Him and trust Him to do so.

15c. They draw away from God because of their sins and failures and wrongs. They actually put distance between themselves and the Lord because they feel so bad about themselves they can't stand to be in His presence.

15d. God's Word convicts us so we will be drawn to Him, not so we will draw away from Him.

15e. Be willing to be changed, to be sanctified — and to ask and trust Him to do it. Then stay out of "works of the flesh" and wait on Him.

15f. Through faith and patience.

16a. It simply means "to make holy."[1]

16b. The God of peace Himself.

16c.   He will fulfill His call upon our lives by hallowing (sanctifying) us and keeping us.

16d.   Believing!

16e.   Sanctification, holiness, purity of mind and heart, the hallowing and keeping of our soul.

16f.   Since it is the Lord Who works all these things in us and for us, He wants the glory to go to Him and not to a set of principles, methods or formulas.

17a.   Nobody had told them to work the works of God; that was their idea. God is big enough to work His own works.

17b.   We hear about the mighty works of God, and immediately our reaction is, "Lord, just show me what I can do to work those works."

17c.   "This is the work that God requires of you, that you believe."

17d.   The way we achieve is to believe. That frees us from worry and reasoning.

Chapter 3

1a.   He wants His children to be free of worry and reasoning.

1b.   To torment oneself with disturbing thoughts; to feel uneasy, anxious or troubled; or, to torment with annoyances, cares or anxieties.[1]

1c.   To seize by the throat with the teeth and shake or mangle.[2]

1d.   The devil tries to steal the peace that was left to us by Jesus by seizing us by the throat and shaking and mangling us until we submit.

1e.   Our enemy does to us — if we allow it to happen.

1f.   The endless revolving of one's mind around and around a situation, searching for knowledge and understanding.

1g.   Although worry is almost always totally negative and pointless because it never produces anything good, sometimes reasoning can seem to be positive and productive.

1h.   We may feel that we have figured out our situation. We may then come into some kind of peace because we think we have worked out a way to handle whatever is bothering us.

1i.   False; trying to solve a problem by leaning on our own understanding rather than leaning on the Lord.

2a.   He means that we are not to think that we have the capacity to figure out everything that is going on in our life.

2b.   Worrying and reasoning.

3a.   Excess.

3b.   Normal; excessive.

3c.   When we get so caught up in details that we lose sight of the big picture. When we become so involved in managing every tiny aspect of our daily lives that we forget to live and enjoy life.

3d.   If you get frustrated and confused, you have gone too far.

3e.   Out of grace and into works.

3f.   Unlikely you are to see the solution to it.

3g.   To follow peace.

3h.   Reasoning does not produce peace. It produces confusion.

4a.   It says to let it ". . . rule (act as umpire continually) in your hearts [deciding and settling with finality all questions that arise in your minds. . .]. . . ."

4b.   Running the mind, trying to figure out what to do.

4c.   (Your answers.)

5a.   Grace and works are diametrically opposed to one another. They cannot fellow-ship or have anything to do with each other.

5b.   Mutually exclusive. The other cannot exist.

5c.   The grace of God ceases to operate on our behalf. God has no choice but to back off and wait until we have finished trying to handle things ourselves.

5d.   Because we are trying to operate without the grace of God — and that is never going to be successful.

5e.   For guidance.

5f.   Not out of the head, but out of the heart, out of "the inner man."

5g.   Discernment is simply God's wisdom for any situation of life. It is a "spiritual knowing" about how to handle things.

5h.   Because the Bible says that God is not the author of confusion, but of peace.

5i.   You open a channel of faith through which He can begin to reveal to you what you need to know in order to handle the problem or situation.

5j.   Speak to it, crying, "Grace, grace!"

5k.   Works; grace.

6a.   Speak to your mountain, but keep your eyes on the Lord.

6b.   He means that we are not to be afraid or intimidated by the size of the obstacle that confronts us in life.

6c.   Through the power of the Holy Spirit, you can face any mountain and remove it from your path.

6d.	When we do that, we are in reality running from the enemy, because he is the one who throws up those obstacles for that very purpose — to cause us to become afraid and give up.

6e.	Because God didn't think we would need it; He never expects us to turn and run away.

6f.	". . . be strong in the Lord, and in the power of his might." We are supposed to know and believe that greater is He Who is in us than he who is in the world.

6g.	The One Who has the answer.

6h.	(Your answer.)

6i.	Because we want to be in control. We have an almost insatiable desire to know. But what we really need is to believe.

6j.	Because we are "workaholics" — we are addicted to worrying and reasoning.

6k.	Obedience.

7a.	To believe.

7b.	Continue in that spirit of obedience and faith by simply doing what God has said.

8.	When our heart is willing to become more and more like Him.

9a.	Letting Him do what He wants to do in this earth through us.

9b.	To be absolutely still mentally, trusting in the Lord rather than worrying or reasoning.

9c.	By really believing in the grace of God.

9d.	Gratitude and thanksgiving?

10a.	Because worry deals with the past, while grace (unmerited favor) deals with the present and the future.

10b.	Trust the grace of God to go back and fix those past mistakes and change our future destiny.

10c.	Rest today, trusting the Lord to take care of our past, our present and our future.

11a.	Because as long as we live we will always have to face situations for which we don't have all the answers.

11b.	No, there will always be something going on in our life that we don't know how to handle; otherwise, we wouldn't need faith, we wouldn't have to trust God.

11c.	By leading us into situations that are over our head.

11d.	Because He already knows exactly what He's going to do. He has got a plan, a path and a work all ready for us.

11e.	The grace.

11f.   A plan; handle everything that we will encounter. Grace; sufficient.

12a.   God is not going to pour out His grace upon us a week ahead of time just so we can wallow in it. Grace is power, and God is not careless with His divine, wonder-working power.

12b.   When we need it and not before.

12c.   That keeps us from feeling so secure in our natural self that we get to thinking we don't need God.

12d.   Increased; decreased.

12e.   Call on the Lord and He will provide you all the grace you need to see you through that challenge to ultimate victory.

13a.   A bad attitude.

13b.   Complaining.

13c.   Sympathy; self-pity.

13d.   Keep.

14a.   To be absolutely still, unmovable, in our decision to wait upon Him to bring about the desired results.

14b.   In God — that is, in His Spirit within us.

14c.   Be a vessel or a channel for God's grace.

15.   We are trying to stand on the flimsiness of the flesh rather than the solidness of the rock.

16a.   Effort cannot eradicate effort, frustration cannot get rid of frustration and care cannot eliminate care.

16b.   By His (God's) grace.

17a.   Grace, grace and more grace all the time in our life. Because where sin abounds, grace does much more abound.

17b.   If our problem gets bigger, God's grace gets bigger. If our problem multiplies, so that we go from one to two or three or more, the grace of God also multiplies so that we are able to handle them.

17c.   Possible with God.

17d.   All.

18a.   A never-ending flow of power.

18b.   His desires, hopes and dreams and ideas will be birthed through us at no cost to us, with no carnal effort on our part. He will be glorified on this earth, and we will have the privilege and the honor of sharing it and being joint-heirs in that glory.

18c. (Your answer.)

19a. He was determined not to know anything but Jesus Christ, and Him crucified.

19b. Because he had discovered that, as the Bible teaches, sometimes knowledge can be aggravating. He had also discovered that knowledge can create pride.

19c. The fact that the natural man does not understand spiritual things.

20a. Two. The mind of the flesh and the mind of the spirit.

20b. We receive information from two different sources.

20c. We get information from our natural mind (which operates without the Holy Spirit), and we get information from our spirit (through which the Holy Spirit communicates directly to us).

21a. We have the mind of Christ. It means that we ". . . hold the thoughts (feelings and purposes) of His heart."

21b. Just off the top of our head.

21c. We are not to be led by our carnal mind, but by the Holy Spirit Who indwells us.

21d. When we get into what *The Amplified Bible* calls "sense and reason without the Holy Spirit." Because the Holy Spirit is the only One Who knows the mind of God.

21e. The problem is that although we have the mind of Christ and know the Word of God, we don't listen to our spirit which is being enlightened by the Holy Spirit. Instead, we listen to our natural mind, which relies strictly on sense and reason without the Holy Spirit.

21f. Out of our spirit and not out of our head.

22a. At our weakest moment, such as when we first get up and are still groggy, half-awake and incoherent.

22b. Satan never moves against strength; he only moves against weakness.

22c. They become ours because in Proverbs 23:7 KJV the Bible says that as we think in our heart, so are we.

22d. They will become reality to us because of our "faith," our belief in them.

22e. Simply take the time to turn to our inner man and say, "Lord, what do You have to say about this?" If we listen in faith, He will speak to us and reveal to us the truth of that situation.

22f. One is carnal information that comes off the top of our head. The other is spiritual information which wells up out of our heart. One is muddy, polluted water, and the other is clean drinking water.

22g. Being double-minded.

22h. It means that your mind is trying to tell you one thing, and your spirit is trying to tell you just the opposite.

22i. We are going to have to decide which fountain of information we are going to drink from. We are going to have to learn to live out of our spirit and not out of our head.

Chapter 4

1a. The fact that despite what happens to us in life, we can have favor with Him and with other people.

1b. Because we never activate our faith in that area.

1c. You must do what Joseph did and believe for it.

1d. He maintained a good attitude in a bad situation. He had a "faith attitude."

2a. First Samuel 2:7.

2b. Because she had favor with Him.

2c. Because she knew that she had favor with God.

2d. Don't try to retaliate by seeking natural favor. Instead, believe God for supernatural favor, because despite how hopeless things may look from a human perspective, God can lift up and He can bring down.

2e. Believe that God is causing everyone you come in contact with to like you, to want to be around you, to look upon you with favor.

3a. Because usually the harder you try to please everyone, the more mistakes you make and the less people are attracted to you.

3b. Win natural favor.

3c. Grace.

3d. They are both translated from the same Greek word *charis*.[1] So the grace of God is the favor of God. And the favor of God is the grace of God.

3e. That which causes things to happen in our life that need to happen, through the channel of our faith. It is the power of God coming through our faith to do what we cannot do on our own.

3f. By God's Spirit of grace.

3g. Favor is the acceptance and blessing that others show toward us because we have God's grace shining upon us.

3h. It relieves the stress that builds up on you.

4a. Natural favor can be earned, supernatural favor can't.

4b. He wants us to devote our time and energy to doing His will, whether it is popular or not.

4c.   Supernatural favor. It cannot be earned; it is a gift, and the way we get it is simply by believing for it and receiving it from God.

4d.   Because it is so fleeting.

4e.   Maintain it the same way you got it.

4f.   Supernatural favor does not depend upon pleasing people all the time. It depends upon God's grace to give acceptance and maintain it.

4g.   It creates within us a thankful and grateful heart.

4h.   We are always more grateful for what we know we don't deserve than we are for what we think we do deserve. That is human nature.

5a.   Because the Lord gave Daniel favor (compassion and loving-kindness) with the eunuch.

5b.   Because the favor of the Lord rested on Daniel and his friends so strongly.

5c.   (Your answer.)

6a.   ". . . in wisdom (in broad and full understanding) and in stature and years, and in favor with God and man."

6b.   "Never have we heard anyone talk like this man!"

6c.   ". . . Have nothing to do with that just and upright Man. . . ."

6d.   ". . . I am not guilty of nor responsible for this righteous Man's blood; see to it yourselves."

6e.   ". . . Indeed, without question, this Man was upright (just and innocent)!"

6f.   After His death.

6g.   As the favored of the Lord.

6h.   He doesn't see us as weak, helpless, sinful creatures. He sees us robed in righteousness, shod with the shoes of peace, wearing the full armor of God and wielding the sword of the Spirit, which is the Word of the Lord.

6i.   Because He looks at us not as we are in the physical realm, but as we are in the spiritual realm.

6j.   When you do that, you are looking at things in the natural; you are not giving the Lord any credit for what He can do.

7a.   Because she found favor in his eyes.

7b.   He watched over her, gave her food and water and instructed his harvesters not only to guard and protect her, but also to leave some extra grain behind for her to pick up.

7c.   Boaz later asked her to marry him. As a result, she and her mother-in-law Naomi were well taken care of for the rest of their lives.

7d. The effects of God's favor upon a person. That same favor is available to us if we will stop trying to get favor by works of our flesh, simply ask for supernatural favor and receive it by faith.

8a. We are sowing seeds for a future harvest of supernatural favor.

8b. On the right track that leads to good, solid, godly relationships.

9a. To be favored is to be featured.

9b. No, not if that favored, featured position comes from God and not from our own personal ambitions or our own selfish efforts to call attention to ourselves.

9c. He singles out that person for special attention and preferential treatment — especially in the presence of others.

9d. It happens to all of us at one time or another, particularly those of us who expect it to happen and even ask God to cause it to happen.

9e. Because it provokes genuine praise and thanksgiving.

9f. We won't ask.

9g. Because we don't feel worthy.

9h. When we are absolutely desperate, when we have gotten ourselves into a situation that we cannot possibly handle on our own.

9i. Cause someone else to do the same for us.

9j. Allow the Lord to shine His light upon us — for His glory.

10a. It means to be particularly favored, esteemed and preferred. It means to enjoy special attention, personal affection and preferential treatment, even without being deserving of it.

10b. He chooses us by an act of His sovereign grace. All we can do is to receive His gracious gift in an attitude of thanksgiving and humility.

10c. Because God is God of all His creation, and because He has a personal relationship with each one of His children.

10d. Because He wants us to be secure in who we are in Christ Jesus so that we will have the confidence and assurance we need to walk victoriously through this life drawing others to share with us in His marvelous grace.

11a. He has chosen man and crowned him with glory and honor.

11b. "Honor," "glory" and "crowned."

11c. "Honor" and "favor."

11d. We might say that God has crowned man with glory and favor, giving him dominion over the works of His hand, and placing all things under his feet.

11e. As the excellencies of God.

11f. That we have been singled out by God Who has placed upon our heads His crown of favor and excellence.

11g. Because we don't believe we deserve them or because we have not been taught they are ours. Our faith is not activated in this area.

11h. Because all things have been placed under our feet by God Who has given us dominion over all His creation.

11i. That which makes something shine.

11j. Respectful regard, esteem, reputation, exalted fame.

11k. Not only will our faces shine forth with the glory of the Lord, but we ourselves will enjoy respect, esteem, a good reputation and fame — all of which are a result of God's favor.

12a. Physically; spiritually.

12b. There just seems to be something about us that causes them to want to show us favor.

12c. Reward.

12d. The light of the Lord was shining upon you.

12e. To give God the thanks and praise.

13a. That He increased in favor with God and man.

13b. The same honor and glory that His Father had given to Him, so that we may be one as They are One.

13c. That we have favor with everyone we meet and in every situation we encounter in life.

13d. That His favor upon us is growing and increasing as we continue to commune with Him and with each other — walking together as one in humble obedience to His will, just as Jesus did.

14a. That God wants us — and through us, everyone on earth — to be in favor with Him.

14b. The devil has stolen it through deceit and delusion.

14c. To restore favor to God's people — and through us to everyone everywhere.

14d. Inheritance. Ministry; unmerited favor.

14e. Ambassadors; emissaries.

14f. Royally.

14g. Kings; priests. Royal ambassadors; divine diplomats.

15a. Timid; doubtful. Who we are in Christ, fully persuaded that we have a right to be doing what we are doing.

15b. Natural; spiritual.

15c. Grace and favor that God has bestowed upon you. Rightful position as a child of God. Right and authority to frighten and intimidate you.

16a. "An evil report."

16b. A good report.

16c. The ten were looking at the situation in the natural, through the eyes of the flesh, while Caleb and Joshua were looking at it in the spiritual, through the eyes of the Lord.

16d. "There we saw the Nephilim [or giants], the sons of Anak, who come from the giants; and we were in our own sight as grasshoppers, and so we were in their sight."

16e. (Your answers.)

16f. The giants; God.

16g. God. God.

16h. You have to be in agreement with His plan for your life. You have to quit seeing yourself as just the opposite of what He says you are. You must learn to change your self-image.

16i. Carry.

16j. On your head a crown of glory and honor.

16k. It means that you have authority. What you say, the Lord will back up.

16l. The righteousness of God in Christ Jesus.

17a. Will humble themselves and allow Him to work His will and way through them.

17b. God can lift up, and He can bring down.

17c. That the power is not ours, it is God's. He doesn't choose us because we are able, but simply because we are available.

18a. We are Christ's ambassadors, personal representatives of the Son of the Living God.

18b. That means that whatever we do, we need to do it with excellence. That means that wherever we go, we are to represent Jesus Christ to everyone we meet, to all we come in contact with.

18c. He appeals to the world, begging them for His sake to lay hold of the divine favor offered them and be reconciled to God the Father.

18d. He is saying that since we have received divine favor, our task, our calling, is to influence others to receive that same divine favor that the Lord wants to impart to them just as He did to us.

19a. It is His face, His appearance.

19b. "May others see God's glory shining upon you and through you."

19c. Putting a smile on your face. God's glory.

19d. Receive favor, because we are told that whatever we sow is what we will reap.

20a. Pray for supernatural favor for yourself from all those you come in contact with and for others to enjoy God's favor.

20b. He would bless him and make him a blessing.

20c. The Bible says there will be times when believers will be persecuted. We must keep every message in balance.

20d. Just pray and ask the Lord to help you stand the pressure, keep a good attitude and bring honor and glory to Him.

20e. Supernatural favor will rest upon you and you will be blessed to be a blessing.

Chapter 5

1a. He desires a thankful people, not a murmuring, grumbling, fault-finding, complaining people.

1b. Unbelief.

1c. That joy and peace are found in believing, not in murmuring, grumbling, fault-finding, or complaining.

1d. A revelation of the grace of God.

2a. That if a person works for his wages, then when payday comes around he is not really appreciative of what he receives because he feels that he deserves it since he has earned it.

2b. The rewards of his own works. Revelation of the grace of God that has been freely poured out upon him.

2c. We will have a proud, self-righteous attitude that will cause us to look down on and judge others who don't seem to be as blessed as we are.

2d. "If those people would just do what I'm doing, then they wouldn't be having all those problems."

2e. "I am what I am by the grace of God."

3a. The Spirit of grace; God's power coming into our life to meet every evil tendency that we have and to help us solve every problem that we encounter.

3b. Every good thing that comes to us in this life comes by the grace of God.

3c. Selfishness; ingratitude.

3d. Humble attitude. Unappreciative; presumptuous.

3e. All complaining does is open the door for the enemy. It doesn't solve problems; it just creates a breeding ground for greater problems.

3f. By developing an attitude of gratitude.

3g. Continual lifestyle of thanksgiving.

4a. By saying, "Father, I thank You that You have heard me."

4b. Because when we know that God has heard us, we know that He has granted our requests.

4c. By lifting up the voice of thanksgiving.

4d. Because there is no powerful living apart from a life of thanksgiving.

4e. A life of thanksgiving.

4f. On many occasions and for many things.

5a. By following a lifestyle of thanksgiving.

5b. For what He has already done.

5c. Act; attitude.

5d. Praise; thanksgiving; petitions.

5e. Grateful heart; mature enough to receive other blessings.

5f. What He does; Who He is.

6a. Grace. Because he knew that it is by God's grace that we receive every good thing that He chooses to bestow upon us.

6b. We get into the bad habit of taking them for granted.

6c. Because we never have to do without them.

6d. On purpose.

7a. That He is going to destroy all their enemies and give them a great victory by pouring out upon them His Spirit of grace (or unmerited favor) and supplication.

7b. Grace; supplication.

7c. Because the Spirit of supplication is a Spirit of prayer, of asking God for what we need rather than trying to make it happen on our own.

7d. It is the message of the power of God coming to us, free, just for believing it.

7e. Come fearlessly, confidently and boldly to God's throne of grace.

8. Live under the Law; perfection. Throne of grace (the throne of His unmerited favor to us).

9a. Because our lives are not truly submitted to and controlled by the Spirit of grace and supplication.

9b. Total dependence upon the Lord.

9c. God Himself will not permit us to succeed. He will block us or oppose us — until we give in, humble ourselves and come to Him saying, "Father, I can't work out this situation; if You want it done, You will have to do it Yourself."

9d. That kind of manipulation, like any other work, only produces frustration.

9e. By truly casting all our cares upon the Lord, asking Him to work them out as He sees best — and then trusting Him to do so.

10a. The Holy Spirit. By simply asking in faith and trust.

10b. To keep on asking, seeking and knocking, on a continual basis, day in and day out, seven days a week, fifty-two weeks a year, so we may keep receiving what we are in need of.

10c. Failing to ask and seek and knock, failing to trust God, our loving heavenly Father, to give us all the good things that we have asked of Him.

10d. In Matthew 7:11 He says that our heavenly Father will give good gifts to those who ask Him. In Luke 11:13 He says that our heavenly Father will give the Holy Spirit to those who ask Him.

10e. His own Holy Spirit.

10f. To bring forth in our lives everything that we need.

10g. Ask.

10h. He meant that the Holy Spirit has a present-day ministry and that the Holy Spirit, the Comforter, the Gift of God, would come to them and abide with them and in them.

11a. The Holy Spirit is a Person, the Third Person of the Trinity. The Holy Spirit is a gift from God bestowed upon us by His grace, requested by us in prayer, and received by us through the channel of faith.

11b. As Comforter, Counselor, Helper, Intercessor, Advocate, Strengthener and Standby.

11c. To get right in the middle of our lives and make them all work out for the glory of God.

12a. Get us ready for that place.

12b. He is the Sanctifier, the agent of sanctification in our life.

12c. Because the Holy Spirit is the power of God given to us to do in us and through us and for us and to us what we could never do on our own.

13a. That of Helper.

13b. (Your answers.)

13c. False.

13d. Because the Holy Spirit is a gentleman; He will not interfere in our personal business without an invitation. He does not knock down our door; instead, He waits to be asked to come in and take charge.

14a. It refers to airline passengers who travel "standby," meaning that they stand by the airline ticket counter waiting to step up and claim a seat on the first available flight.

14b. The Holy Spirit is One Who stands by us at all times waiting for the first available opportunity to jump in and give us the help and strength we need — which is why He is also called our Helper, our Strengthener.

14c. "Help!"

14d. Because it is a vital part of His ministry to help and strengthen those who serve the Lord. He is sent to minister grace to us.

14e. Because we are not receiving the help and strength that the Holy Spirit is constantly reaching out to give us.

14f. By availing ourselves of that ever-present Source of help and strength.

14g. That they will renew their strength.

14h. That of Teacher, Guide or Counselor.

15a. To represent Jesus and act on His behalf, to teach us all things and to cause us to recall everything the Lord has told us.

15b. No, it means that we need to be led by the Holy Spirit, even in seeking counsel and advice from other people.

15c. The Holy Spirit. "Holy Spirit, teach me, counsel me."

15d. Leave it with Him. Don't go on trying to handle it in your own strength and wisdom. It won't work. It will only lead to more misery and frustration.

15e. Guide you into all truth.

16a. His own peace.

16b. Because we will try to live by works rather than by grace.

16c. We must put aside our works and rely totally upon God's grace. We must trust His Holy Spirit as our Counselor Who will lead us into all truth and bring all things to our remembrance, giving us holy recall.

16d. To trust all that to the Holy Spirit Who will guide us and direct us.

16e. Enjoy more success.

16f. Fellowshipping.

17a. That we may have close fellowship with Him and He with us.

17b. To take *The Amplified Bible* and intently study every one of the words in John 16:7-11 describing the ministry of the Holy Spirit, asking yourself, "Am I allowing the Holy Spirit to be my personal Comforter, Counselor, Helper, Advocate, Intercessor, Strengthener and Standby, or am I trying to be all these things on my own. Am I depending upon God's grace, or my efforts." Come into close fellowship with the Holy Spirit.

17c. She suggests saying, "Father, I pray that I will receive the ministry of Your Holy Spirit today, in all His fullness. Whatever I need, I ask You to provide for me through the presence and power of Your Spirit Who is with me and lives in me. In Jesus' name I pray, amen."

18a. Although we have to do the asking, it is God's power that does the doing.

18b. To be with us and to live in us and minister to us — so we will know what to ask.

18c. By doing a whole lot more asking.

18d. Ask and ask and ask. Keep on asking, so that you may receive, and your joy may be full.

19a. How we are to react to the various trials and temptations that we all encounter in life.

19b. They bring out our endurance and steadfastness and patience.

19c. Let them do a thorough work in us so that we will come through them stronger and better than we were before.

19d. We are not to worry and fret or run to others, but rather to ask.

19e. We are to ask "the giving God" because His nature is to give. He gives without finding fault with us.

19f. We are to ask "in faith" because ". . . without faith it is impossible to please and be satisfactory to Him."

19g. We are to ask in faith without doubting. We should make up our minds what we believe and not be double-minded about it.

19h. A "giving God." "Liberally and ungrudgingly." "To everyone." "Without reproaching or fault-finding."

19i. We could say, "If you are deficient in wisdom, ask of the giving God, Who gives to everyone liberally, without scolding or criticizing sharply for mistakes, because He wants to help you, even when you haven't done everything exactly right."

19j. Because if we did, we wouldn't be dependent upon Him any more. There would be no more need for His grace and mercy.

19k. No. It just means that we will never fully reach it until He returns to take us home to be with Him.

20a. Life of power.

20b. A "tale" or a "narration," a telling of something that has gone on in a person's life. It is "the genuine confession of facts in one's life which gives glory to God."[1]

20c. We will be so amazed that we will always have a tale to tell about the marvelous things He is doing for us — things that we don't deserve.

20d. Offering up to God a sacrifice of praise, the fruit of our lips that thankfully acknowledge and confess and glorify His name.

Chapter 6

1a. He meant that he did not try to substitute his owns works for the gift of God's grace.

1b. He says that he is what he is, not by his own efforts, but by God's grace. That that grace was not bestowed upon him in vain.

1c. It means "useless" or "to no purpose." God does not pour out His grace upon us for no reason or without a real goal in mind.

1d. Not just so we can enjoy it, but so we can be empowered to do something with it.

1e. Live a holy life.

2a. Holy just as He is holy.

2b. Basically, *holiness* is "separation to God," a separation that should result in "conduct befitting those so separated."[1]

2c. Saints, another word used to describe those who are holy.

2d. To represent the Holy One Who has called us out of the world and separated us unto Himself for His design and purpose.

3a. He is called holy because that is what He is, and His purpose in taking up residence in us is to make us holy too.

3b. To help us to fulfill His design and purpose for us.

3c. Sanctification.

4a. To the process that God uses to do a work in us by His indwelling Holy Spirit to make us more and more holy until finally we become just like His Son Jesus.

4b. Are we making progress toward holiness, are we cooperating with the Holy Spirit and allowing Him to do what He wants to do in our life?

4c. Serious. We are to recognize that it is God's will for us. We are to desire it with all our heart. We are to make every effort to cooperate with the Holy Spirit Who is working to bring it to pass in us day by day.

4d. Sin.

5a. A license to sin.

5b. They reasoned, "Well, then, if the more we sin, the more grace abounds, and if God takes such delight in giving us His grace, then we ought to sin as much as we can so we can get more grace!"

5c. "God forbid! Don't you know that when you sin you become a servant to sin? How can you go on living in sin when you have been declared dead to sin?"

5d. Sin; grace.

5e. Empower us to live a holy life.

6a. We should get holier and holier and holier.

6b. The mistake of thinking that grace is just an excuse to stay the way we are, claiming that we don't have to do anything about ourselves and our lives because we are not under the Law but under grace.

6c. To live as God intends for us to live — which is in holiness.

6d. Lift us out of sin.

6e. To help us understand and live by the marvelous grace of God.

7a. Through the Holy Spirit.

7b. Through His power.

7c. To reveal to us the Truth.

7d. Turn that word back to Him and depend upon Him to give us the power to accomplish it.

7e. Because it causes people to go out and start trying to live a holy life without knowing how to do what they know they should be doing.

7f. The key is to know what is God's part and what is our part. That knowledge is revealed to us by the indwelling Holy Spirit, the Spirit of Truth, if we are willing to listen and learn.

8a. Everything about us — not only our possessions, our money and time and energy and efforts — but also our bodies, our heads and hands and tongues — even our minds and emotions, our attitudes.

8b. Let our countenance show forth His glory and praise.

8c. All; living sacrifice; service; spiritual worship.

8d. Mind.

8e. Our mind and will.

8f. Resting; passive.

8g. Care; responsibility.

8h. Us; the Holy Spirit.

9a. As "separation to God," a separation that should result in "conduct befitting those so separated."[2]

9b. "Cannot be transferred or imputed."[3] That means that holiness is an individual possession, one that is built up little by little. It cannot be given to or taken from another person.

9c. It means that we cannot become holy by going through a prayer line or by having hands laid on us or by associating with someone else who is holy.

9d. Unholiness; holiness.

10a. They try to live by somebody else's convictions about holiness.

10b. Individual.

10c. Do what others are doing or telling us to do just because they believe it is God's will for them.

10d. Make others do what we are doing just because God has convicted us that it is His will for us.

10e. Our lack of acceptance of them as they are hurts our personal relationships, and they feel rejected and criticized.

10f. God. From a heart of "want to" — not "have to."

10g. Letting other people put their convictions off on you or putting your convictions off on them. The Bible says that we are to be led by the prompting of the Holy Spirit,[4] and the Holy Spirit is given to each of us individually for that very purpose.

10h. They can't or won't content themselves with hearing and following the Holy Spirit for themselves — and then allowing others the same right and privilege. They think that everybody in the Body of Christ has got to be doing the same thing the same way at the same time for the same reason.

10i. Setting our own house in order. We need to mind our own business!

10j. God deals with each of us in His own way and in His own time. We are all at different stages of sanctification, which is a process that is worked out by the Holy Spirit in a unique way in each individual believer.

10k. It will hinder our own progress.

10l.   Learn to take care of our own affairs and leave the criticizing and judging of others to God.

11a.   Give an account of our own self to Him.

11b.   To work on our own sanctification and quit putting stumbling blocks, obstacles and hindrances in the way of our brothers and sisters in Christ.

11c.   To follow our own convictions — and let everyone else do the same.

12a.   Keep your personal convictions to yourself. Don't go around trying to put them off on everybody else.

12b.   That is not our job.

12c.   That it is not us, but it is the Holy Spirit Who is the Helper.

12d.   Whether what we are about to do is God's idea or ours. We have to be sure of our true motivation.

12e.   ". . . not to estimate and think of himself more highly than he ought [not to have an exaggerated opinion of his own importance] . . . ."

12f.   God's grace; fleshly zeal.

12g.   Because he is not acting in faith, he is not being true to his personal convictions.

12h.   It means that whatever is done without a personal, inner conviction of its approval by God is sinful.

12i.   Instead of leading him to faith, we may be doing just the opposite; we may be causing him to sin because he is trying to operate off of our personal convictions rather than his own God-approved convictions.

13a.   That as we get into the Word of God we are transformed into His image, going from glory to glory.

13b.   That we have not yet arrived at the full state of holiness.

13c.   Process of sanctification; "the separation of the believer from the world."[5]

13d.   "State into which God, in grace, calls sinful men."[6]

13e.   "Little by little."

13f.   Step by step.

13g.   By the highway of grace.

14a.   ". . . work out your own salvation with fear and trembling."

14b.   He means that we are to cooperate fully with God by cultivating that seed of holiness that has been sown in us.

14c.   With the water of the Word.

14d.   It begins to grow within us and to spread its branches to every part of our being.

14e. It means becoming like Him in every way.

14f. Don't become discouraged. Keep pressing on even if you progress only inch by inch — it is still progress.

15a. Not in our own strength, but by the power of the Holy Spirit Who is at work within us to create in us both the will and the ability to do what pleases the Father.

15b. We receive the gift of God's Holy Spirit Who comes to take up residence within us. Then as we submit ourselves to Him, He works within us, causing us to want to do the will of God, and providing us the strength and power to do that will.

16a. The Word.

16b. The Holy Spirit.

16c. There is a missing part — and that part is the Spirit.

16d. Be yielded to the Holy Spirit within us Who has been given to us to empower us to be able to do the Word.

16e. Because it alone has the power to save our souls.

16f. By reaching out to God in faith and thanksgiving, leaning entirely on Him and relying completely on Him, allowing His Word and Holy Spirit to bring you through the process of sanctification to purity and holiness.

17a. A refiner's fire and fullers' soap.

17b. Fire.

17c. Fullers' soap.

18a. Bring conviction of sin, righteousness and judgment.

18b. Refines, purifies and sanctifies us by cleansing us of our sins.

18c. By the Spirit and the Word, by the application of soap and water.

18d. We try to remove the spots of sin on our souls by relying on our own efforts instead of being patient and allowing the Lord to remove them by soap and water — by His Spirit and His Word.

18e. We apply more soap and let it soak overnight. We apply grace, grace and more grace. Not more scrubbing, not more effort, but more power is what is needed.

19a. (Your answer.)

19b. Sprinkling a little dab of guilt and remorse and condemnation on the problem.

19c. She has received a lot of revelation about grace!

19d. She repents. She opens up the channel of faith and asks the Lord to pour grace through that channel. She asks Him to guard her from the sin of presumption, to keep her from jumping to conclusions and judging things and people before she has all the facts.

19e. Through faith and patience.

19f. Because we have not yet learned to trust God enough to keep us from sinning. Then once we do fall into sin, we are miserable because we feel that we have once again failed ourselves and Him. We hate what we have done and the fact that we don't have the ability to keep ourselves from doing it.

19g. Grace.

19h. That God's grace is always sufficient to meet every weakness.

19i. Grace, grace and more grace.

Conclusion

1. Because her entire Christian experience was a struggle before she learned about grace.

2. As "the missing link" in the faith walk.

3. Because those of us who are addicted to our own works and efforts usually need several applications of the message on grace to bring healing in our approach to life.

4. That the grace of God is the exact opposite of works of the flesh and that when you feel frustrated it is because you have entered into your own effort and need to get back into God's grace.

5. Easy; hard; impossible.

6a. That if we will come to Him, He will give us rest.

6b. Grace, grace and more grace.

Endnotes

Introduction

[1] See 1 Corinthians 1:4.

Chapter 1

[1] Based on definitions in *Webster's New World Dictionary*, 3rd college ed., s.v. "frustrate."

Chapter 2

[1] *Webster's*, s.v. "sanctify."

Chapter 3

[1] Based on definitions from *Webster's*, s.v. "worry."

[2] Based on definitions from *Webster's*, s.v. "worry."

Chapter 4

[1] James Strong, *Strong's Exhaustive Concordance of the Bible* (Nashville: Abingdon, 1890), "Greek Dictionary of the New Testament," p. 77, entry #5485.

Chapter 5

[1] W.E. Vine, *Vine's Expository Dictionary of Old and New Testament Words* (Old Tappan: Fleming H. Revell Company, 1981), Vol. 3: Lo-Ser, p. 198.

Chapter 6

[1] Vine, Vol. 2: E-Li, p. 225.

[2] Vine, Vol. 2: E-Li, p. 225.

[3] Vine, Vol. 3: Lo-Ser, p. 317.

[4] See John 16:13; Romans 8:14; Galatians 5:18.

[5] Vine, Vol. 3: Lo-Ser, p. 318.

[6] Vine, Vol. 3: Lo-Ser, pp. 317, 318.

About the Author

Joyce Meyer has been teaching the Word of God since 1976 and in full-time ministry since 1980. Previously the associate pastor at Life Christian Church in St. Louis, Missouri, she developed, coordinated, and taught a weekly meeting known as "Life In The Word." After more than five years, the Lord brought it to a conclusion, directing her to establish her own ministry and call it *"Life In The Word, Inc."*

Now, her *Life In The Word* radio and television broadcasts are seen and heard by millions across the United States and throughout the world. Joyce's teaching tapes are enjoyed internationally, and she travels extensively conducting *Life In The Word* conferences.

Joyce and her husband, Dave, the business administrator at *Life In The Word*, have been married for over 35 years. They reside in St. Louis, Missouri, and are the parents of four children. All four children are married and, along with their spouses, work with Dave and Joyce in the ministry.

Believing the call on her life is to establish believers in God's Word, Joyce says, "Jesus died to set the captives free, and far too many Christians have little or no victory in their daily lives." Finding herself in the same situation many years ago and having found freedom to live in victory through applying God's Word, Joyce goes equipped to set captives free and to exchange ashes for beauty. She believes that every person who walks in victory leads many others into victory. Her life is transparent, and her teachings are practical and can be applied in everyday life.

Joyce has taught on emotional healing and related subjects in meetings all over the country, helping multiplied thousands. She has recorded more than 225 different audiocassette albums and over 100 videos. She has also authored 49 books to help the body of Christ on various topics.

Her "Emotional Healing Package" contains over 23 hours of teaching on the subject. Albums included in this package are: "Confidence"; "Beauty for

Ashes" (includes Joyce's teaching notes); "Managing Your Emotions"; "Bitterness, Resentment, and Unforgiveness"; "Root of Rejection"; and a 90-minute Scripture/music tape titled "Healing the Brokenhearted."

Joyce's "Mind Package" features five different audio tape series on the subject of the mind. They include: "Mental Strongholds and Mindsets"; "Wilderness Mentality"; "The Mind of the Flesh"; "The Wandering, Wondering Mind"; and "Mind, Mouth, Moods, and Attitudes." The package also contains Joyce's powerful book, *Battlefield of the Mind*. On the subject of love she has three tape series titled "Love Is..."; "Love: The Ultimate Power"; and "Loving God, Loving Yourself, and Loving Others," and a book titled *Reduce Me to Love*.

Write to Joyce Meyer's office for a resource catalog and further information on how to obtain the tapes you need to bring total healing to your life.

To contact the author write:

Joyce Meyer Ministries
P. O. Box 655
Fenton, Missouri 63026

or call: (636) 349-0303

Internet Address: www.joycemeyer.org

Please include your testimony or help received from this book when you write. Your prayer requests are welcome.

To contact the author
in Canada, please write:

Joyce Meyer Ministries Canada, Inc.
Lambeth Box 1300
London, ON N6P 1T5

or call: (636) 349-0303

In Australia, please write:

Joyce Meyer Ministries-Australia
Locked Bag 77
Mansfield Delivery Centre
Queensland 4122

or call: 07 3349 1200

In England, please write:

Joyce Meyer Ministries
P. O. Box 1549
Windsor
SL4 1GT

or call: (0) 1753-831102

Books by Joyce Meyer

Teenagers Are People Too!

Filled with the Spirit

A Celebration of Simplicity

The Joy of Believing Prayer

Never Lose Heart

Being the Person God Made You to Be

A Leader in the Making

"Good Morning, This Is God!" Gift Book

JESUS – Name Above All Names

"Good Morning, This Is God!" Daily Calendar

Help Me – I'm Married!

Reduce Me to Love

Be Healed in Jesus' Name

How to Succeed at Being Yourself

Eat and Stay Thin

Weary Warriors, Fainting Saints

Life in the Word Journal

Life in the Word Devotional

Be Anxious for Nothing

Be Anxious for Nothing Study Guide

The Help Me! Series:
I'm Alone!
I'm Stressed! • I'm Insecure!
I'm Discouraged! • I'm Depressed!
I'm Worried! • I'm Afraid!

Don't Dread

Managing Your Emotions

Healing the Brokenhearted

"Me and My Big Mouth!"

"Me and My Big Mouth!" Study Guide

Prepare to Prosper

Do It! Afraid

*Expect a Move of God in Your Life . . . **Suddenly***

Enjoying Where You Are on the Way to Where You Are Going

The Most Important Decision You'll Ever Make

When, God, When?

Why, God, Why?

The Word, the Name, the Blood

Battlefield of the Mind

Battlefield of the Mind Study Guide

Tell Them I Love Them

Peace

The Root of Rejection

Beauty for Ashes

If Not for the Grace of God

New: *If Not for the Grace of God Study Guide*

By Dave Meyer
Nuggets of Life
Available from your local bookstore.

Harrison House
Tulsa, Oklahoma 74153
www.harrisonhouse.com

The Harrison House Vision

Proclaiming the truth and the power

Of the Gospel of Jesus Christ

With excellence;

Challenging Christians to

Live victoriously,

Grow spiritually,

Know God intimately.